The Essential Buyer's Guide

PORSCHE
911 (997)

2nd generation: model years 2009 to 2012

Your marque expert:
Adrian Streather

T0386786

VELOCE PUBLISHING
THE PUBLISHER OF FINE AUTOMOTIVE BOOKS

Alfa Romeo Alfasud (Metcalfe)
Alfa Romeo Alfetta: all saloon/
 sedan models 1972 to 1984 &
 coupé models 1974 to 1987
 (Metcalfe)
Alfa Romeo Giulia GT Coupé
 (Booker)
Alfa Romeo Giulia Spider (Booker)
Audi TT (Davies)
Audi TT Mk2 2006 to 2014
 (Durnan)
Austin-Healey Big Healeys
 (Trummel)
BMW Boxer Twins (Henshaw)
BMW E30 3 Series 1981 to 1994
 (Hosier)
BMW GS (Henshaw)
BMW X5 (Saunders)
BMW Z3 Roadster (Fishwick)
BMW Z4: E85 Roadster and E86
 Coupé including M and Alpina
 2003 to 2009 (Smitheram)
BSA 350, 441 & 500 Singles
 (Henshaw)
BSA 500 & 650 Twins (Henshaw)
BSA Bantam (Henshaw)
Choosing, Using & Maintaining
 Your Electric Bicycle (Henshaw)
Citroën 2CV (Paxton)
Citroën DS & ID (Heilig)
Cobra Replicas (Ayre)
Corvette C2 Sting Ray 1963-1967
 (Falconer)
Datsun 240Z 1969 to 1973 (Newlyn)
DeLorean DMC-12 1981 to 1983
 (Williams)
Ducati Bevel Twins (Falloon)
Ducati Desmodue Twins (Falloon)
Ducati Desmoquattro Twins – 851,
 888, 916, 996, 998, ST4 1988 to
 2004 (Falloon)
FIAT 124 Spider & Pininfarina
 Azzura Spider, (AS-DS) 1966 to
 1985 (Robertson)
Fiat 500 & 600 (Bobbitt)
Ford Capri (Paxton)
Ford Escort Mk1 & Mk2
 (Williamson)
Ford Focus Mk1 RS & ST170, 1st
 Generation (Williamson)
Ford Model A – All Models 1927 to
 1931 (Buckley)
Ford Model T – All models 1909 to
 1927 (Barker)
Ford Mustang – First Generation
 1964 to 1973 (Cook)
Ford Mustang – 3rd generation:
 1979-1993; inc Mercury Capri:
 1979-1986 (Smith)
Ford Mustang – Fifth Generation

(2005-2014) (Cook)
Ford RS Cosworth Sierra & Escort
 (Williamson)
Harley-Davidson Big Twins
 (Henshaw)
Hillman Imp (Morgan)
Hinckley Triumph triples & fours
 750, 900, 955, 1000, 1050, 1200
 – 1991-2009 (Henshaw)
Honda CBR FireBlade (Henshaw)
Honda CBR600 Hurricane
 (Henshaw)
Honda SOHC Fours 1969-1984
 (Henshaw)
Jaguar E-Type 3.8 & 4.2 litre
 (Crespin)
Jaguar E-type V12 5.3 litre
 (Crespin)
Jaguar Mark 1 & 2 (All models
 including Daimler 2.5-litre V8)
 1955 to 1969 (Thorley)
Jaguar New XK 2005-2014
 (Thorley)
Jaguar S-Type – 1999 to 2007
 (Thorley)
Jaguar X-Type – 2001 to 2009
 (Thorley)
Jaguar XJ-S (Crespin)
Jaguar XJ6, XJ8 & XJR (Thorley)
Jaguar XK 120, 140 & 150
 (Thorley)
Jaguar XK8 & XKR (1996-2005)
 (Thorley)
Jaguar/Daimler XJ 1994-2003
 (Crespin)
Jaguar/Daimler XJ40 (Crespin)
Jaguar/Daimler XJ6, XJ12 &
 Sovereign (Crespin)
Kawasaki Z1 & Z900 (Orritt)
Lancia Delta HF 4WD & Integrale
 (Baker)
Land Rover Discovery Series 1
 (1989-1998) (Taylor)
Land Rover Discovery Series 2
 (1998-2004) (Taylor)
Land Rover Series I, II & IIA
 (Thurman)
Land Rover Series III (Thurman)
Lotus Elan, S1 to Sprint and Plus
 2 to Plus 2S 130/5 1962 to
 1974 (Vale)
Lotus Europa, S1, S2, Twin-cam &
 Special 1966 to 1975 (Vale)
Lotus Seven replicas & Caterham
 7: 1973-2013 (Hawkins)
Mazda MX-5 Miata (Mk1 1989-97
 & Mk2 98-2001) (Crook)
Mazda MX-5 Miata (Mk3, 3.5 &
 3.75 models, 2005-2015) (Wild)
Mazda RX-8 (Parish)

Mercedes-Benz 190: all 190
 models (W201 series) 1982 to
 1993 (Parish)
Mercedes-Benz 280-560SL &
 SLC (Bass)
Mercedes-Benz G-Wagen
 (Greene)
Mercedes-Benz Pagoda 230SL,
 250SL & 280SL roadsters &
 coupés (Bass)
Mercedes-Benz S-Class W126
 Series (Zoporowski)
Mercedes-Benz S-Class Second
 Generation W116 Series (Parish)
Mercedes-Benz SL R129-series
 1989 to 2001 (Parish)
Mercedes-Benz SLK (Bass)
Mercedes-Benz W123 (Parish)
Mercedes-Benz W124 – All
 models 1984-1997 (Zoporowski)
MG Midget & A-H Sprite (Horler)
MG TD, TF & TF1500 (Jones)
MGA 1955-1962 (Crosier)
MGB & MGB GT (Williams)
MGF & MG TF (Hawkins)
Mini (Paxton)
Morgan 4/4 (Benfield)
Morgan Plus 4 (Benfield)
Morris Minor & 1000 (Newell)
Moto Guzzi 2-valve big twins
 (Falloon)
New Mini (Collins)
Norton Commando (Henshaw)
Peugeot 205 GTI (Blackburn)
Piaggio Scooters – all modern
 two-stroke & four-stroke
 automatic models 1991 to 2016
 (Willis)
Porsche 356 (Johnson)
Porsche 911 (964) (Streather)
Porsche 911 (991) (Streather)
Porsche 911 (993) (Streather)
Porsche 911 (996) (Streather)
Porsche 911 (997) – Model years
 2004 to 2009 (Streather)
Porsche 911 (997) – Second
 generation models 2009 to 2012
 (Streather)
Porsche 911 Carrera 3.2
 (Streather)
Porsche 911SC (Streather)
Porsche 924 – All models 1976 to
 1988 (Hodgkins)
Porsche 928 (Hemmings)
Porsche 930 Turbo & 911 (930)
 Turbo (Streather)
Porsche 944 (Higgins)
Porsche 981 Boxster & Cayman
 (Streather)
Porsche 986 Boxster (Streather)

Porsche 987 Boxster and Cayman
 1st generation
 (2005-2009) (Streather)
Porsche 987 Boxster and Cayman
 2nd generation (2009-2012)
 (Streather)
Range Rover – First Generation
 models 1970 to 1996 (Taylor)
Range Rover – Second Generation
 1994-2001 (Taylor)
Range Rover – Third Generation
 L322 (2002-2012) (Taylor)
Reliant Scimitar GTE (Payne)
Rolls-Royce Silver Shadow &
 Bentley T-Series (Bobbitt)
Rover 2000, 2200 & 3500
 (Marrocco)
Royal Enfield Bullet (Henshaw)
Subaru Impreza (Hobbs)
Sunbeam Alpine (Barker)
Triumph 350 & 500 Twins
 (Henshaw)
Triumph Bonneville (Henshaw)
Triumph Herald & Vitesse (Ayre)
Triumph Spitfire and GT6 (Ayre)
Triumph Stag (Mort)
Triumph Thunderbird, Trophy &
 Tiger (Henshaw)
Triumph TR2 & TR3 - All models
 (including 3A & 3B) 1953 to 1962
 (Conners)
Triumph TR4/4A & TR5/250 - All
 models 1961 to 1968 (Child
 & Battyll)
Triumph TR6 (Williams)
Triumph TR7 & TR8 (Williams)
Triumph Trident & BSA Rocket
 III (Rooke)
TVR Chimaera and Griffith
 (Kitchen)
TVR S-series (Kitchen)
Velocette 350 & 500 Singles 1946
 to 1970 (Henshaw)
Vespa Scooters – Classic 2-stroke
 models 1960-2008 (Paxton)
Volkswagen Bus (Copping)
Volkswagen Transporter T4 (1990-
 2003) (Copping/Cservenka)
VW Golf GTI (Copping)
VW Beetle (Copping)
Volvo 700/900 Series (Beavis)
Volvo P1800/1800S, E & ES 1961
 to 1973 (Murray)

www.veloce.co.uk

First published in April 2016, reprinted July 2022 by Veloce Publishing Limited, Veloce House, Parkway Farm Business Park, Middle Farm Way, Poundbury, Dorchester, Dorset, DT1 3AR, England.
Fax 01305 250479/Tel 01305 260068/e-mail info@veloce.co.uk/web www.veloce.co.uk or www.velocebooks.com.

ISBN: 978-1-845848-66-8 UPC: 6-36847-04866-2

Readers with ideas for automotive books, or books on other transport or related hobby subjects, are invited to write to the editorial director of Veloce Publishing at the above address.
British Library Cataloguing in Publication Data – A catalogue record for this book is available from the British Library.
Typesetting, design and page make-up all by Veloce Publishing Ltd on Apple Mac.
Printed and bound by CPI Group (UK) Ltd, Croydon, CR0 4YY.

Introduction
– the purpose of this book

The information in this buyer's guide is arranged in user-friendly chapters to allow any prospective road legal 2nd generation 997 purchaser to make informed decisions on whether or not to proceed with a purchase after viewing, inspecting properly and, most importantly, test driving the car.

The 2nd generation Carrera 4 Coupé and 4S Cabriolet are almost totally new cars. (Courtesy Porsche AG archive)

The 2nd generation 997 was created from the same basic chassis platform as the 1st generation 997 models, but, with the exception of the GT models, the differences were immense. The 2nd generation was given the brand new direct fuel injected type MA1 engine series, the brand new PDK 7-speed automatic transmission, and a new all-wheel drive system with enhanced forms of traction control, and these are just some of the highlights to emerge between model years 2009 and 2013. There was also a raft of limited edition models, some produced only by Porsche Exclusive.

The only 2nd generation 997 model produced beyond model year 2012 was the Turbo S, which continued in production for the first two months of model year 2013. (Courtesy Porsche AG archive)

The 2nd generation 997 model range remains a totally unambiguous water-cooled series, with the new Carrera, Carrera 4, Targa 4 and Turbo models having only some structural, and basic, systems in common with the previous 1st generation 997 model range. Much is, at minimum, upgraded, but much is replaced.

The brand new 3.6-litre and 3.8-litre direct fuel-injection (DFI) integrated dry-sump engine installations are a major step away from Porsche engine tradition. Bosch is also gone, with Siemens taking responsibility for engine management and fault diagnostic software.

The 2nd generation Turbo models also travel a new path, receiving a brand new direct fuel injected turbocharged integrated dry-sump oil 3.8-litre engine.

The GT3 and GT3 RS models are fitted with an upgraded 3.8-litre engine, and the GT3 RS receives a 4.0-litre engine, in model year 2011. The GT2 becomes the GT2 RS, but retains its original 3.6-litre – albeit seriously upgraded in the power department.

A brand new 7-speed Porsche Doppelkupplung (PDK) automatic transmission sends the old 5-speed Tiptronic S to the pages of history. The Aisin manual 6-speed transmissions are upgraded, but essentially remain the same as before.

Carrera GTS and Carrera 4 GTS Coupé and Cabriolet bodystyles debut, and the limited edition models are headed up by the 911 Sport Classic with its 1973 style ducktail rear wing (spoiler), and the very limited edition Speedster model.

2nd generation 997 production numbers totalled 76,259 (total production including the 1st generation models is 212,704), but this time the sins of the father can't be passed onto the 2nd son. There are no known major technical issues with any of the 2nd generation 997 models.

The 2nd generation 997 series was produced over four full model years with the 2nd generation 997 Turbo continuing in production into model year 2013.

Owning a pre-loved 2nd generation 997 provides years of motoring pleasure and enjoyment from being part of the Porsche experience, and with no known serious technical problems like it predecessors used 997 purchasers can feel confident in the product far more than in the past. There's little that can potentially ruin the 2nd generation Porsche 997 experience apart from cost of spare parts and the fact that the 2nd generation 997s are hard to work on at home, but it's still possible.

Special thanks to all credited photographic contributors mentioned in this book.

The 2nd generation 997 GT2 RS is an awesome piece of kit straight out of the factory.
(Courtesy Porsche AG archive)

Contents

The Essential Buyer's Guide™ currency
At the time of publication a BG unit of currency "⬤" equals approximately
£1.00/US$1.20/Euro 1.18. Please adjust to suit current exchange rates
using Sterling as the base currency.

– marriage guidance

Tall and short drivers

All 997 models, both left- and right-hand drive, provide a comfortable driving position for short and tall drivers as an adjustable position steering wheel is installed and there's plenty of seat adjustment.

Weight of controls

All 997 models are fitted with power steering, which helps significantly reduce the load on the arms. All 997s, including the GT2 and GT3, are fitted with a vacuum brake boost system, which is very effective even at 335kph (208mph) in a 997 GT2. The double-mass flywheel and hydraulic clutch operating system, fitted to all 997 models (except the 997 GT3 RS with its single-mass flywheel), is generally lighter to operate with far less stress on the left leg than with previous series.

Will it fit the garage?

Measure it and compare, but don't forget the doors have to be opened in the garage. Chapter 17 contains a table with each specific model's dimensions.

Does it fit in the garage? (Author's collection)

Interior space

There's plenty of legroom in the front of a 997 for driver and passenger. However, for some, comfort depends on type of seat installed. The standard comfort seat nicely supports people of average girth width, but sport, bucket and racing seats are designed for those who are not so wide at the hips, and the rear seats are essentially useless.

Luggage capacity

There's sufficient room in the back of a 997, with both rear seat backs down, to carry a lot of luggage. Front luggage compartment capacity is model dependent, and there's no spare wheel and tyre assembly installed in any 997 model – just a spare-tyre-in-a-tin (sealant for minor damage caused by nails, screws or other items that have pierced the tyre).

Running costs

The 997 cost of ownership in every area is lower than its air-cooled ancestors. However, it's still a high powered sports car, designed to be driven, and the resulting cost of ownership is higher than for a standard road car.

Usability

It's a sports car, and none of the 997 models should be driven on snow- and ice-covered roads without proper winter tyres. Various improved driver aids installed in the 997 series do make it safer in harsh conditions, but it still rides low and salt (grit) used on winter roads to clear snow and ice will eat away the metalwork.

Parts availability

2nd generation 997 parts are readily available around the world, albeit some are very expensive.

Parts cost

It's a Porsche – it's a high-performance sports car, expect to pay more for parts. Electronic control units can be extremely expensive, and many other parts are not repairable. The optional ceramic brake disc (rotor) and pad replacements are very expensive, as are some of the new DFI engine spares, such as the high pressure fuel pump and fuel injectors.

Insurance

Check with your insurance company, as a 997 can be very expensive to fully insure. If you cannot afford full insurance coverage, you shouldn't purchase it.

Investment potential

The 997 offers great bang for your buck in the sports car market, but do not expect to make a profit on resale, except possibly with some of the limited edition models.

Foibles

No adjustment in the suspension, except for GT models.
No underside protection of the engine.
Carrying out DIY (home) engine and transmission repairs very difficult.
Unique centre-lock wheels on some models can cause roadside removal issues.

Plus points

Every girl loves a Porsche.
Porsche sports exhaust system available for retrofit.
Factory aerodynamic body, lowering and sports suspension kits available for retrofit.
Ownership costs are lower than for its ancestors.
Limited edition models available, especially for those with deep pockets.

Minus points

System complexity.
Patchy customer support.
Software upgrades can be costly.
Spare part costs.

Alternatives

1st generation Porsche 911 (997), Porsche 911 (991), Porsche 987 Boxster or Cayman, Porsche 981 Boxster or Cayman, BMW M3 and Ferrari 430.

2 Cost considerations
– affordable, or a money pit?

Service by an approved Porsche dealer
Intervals: Every 20,000 miles or 30,000km (intermediate) and 40,000 miles or 60,000km (maintenance) model years 2009 to 2013 inclusive.
Minor service cost: from ●x450
Major service cost: from ●x800

Mechanical parts cost
Secondhand 3.6-litre MA1.02 engine: from ●x13,000
Secondhand 3.8-litre MA1.01 engine: from ●x18,000
Secondhand 3.8-litre M97.77 engine: from ●x25,000

Simple DIY servicing reduces ownership costs considerably.
(Courtesy David Yusem)

Secondhand 3.8-litre MA1.70 turbocharged engine: from ●x30,000
Secondhand G97.05 manual transmission: from ●x4000
Secondhand G97.35 manual transmission: from ●x6000
Secondhand G97.55 manual transmission: from ●x8000
Secondhand G97.90/92 manual transmission: from ●x10,000
Secondhand G97.88 manual transmission: from ●x12,000
Secondhand CG1.00 PDK transmission: from ●x5000
Secondhand CG1.30 PDK transmission: from ●x7000
Secondhand CG1.50 PDK transmission: from ●x9000
Clutch kit: ●x475

Porsche communication management (PCM) system 997 style. (Courtesy Joe Ramos)

Steel brake discs (rotors) front (pair): ●x250
Steel brake discs (rotors) rear (pair): ●x250
Brake pads front for steel (pair): ●x180
Brake pads rear for steel (pair): ●x100
Ceramic brake discs (rotors) front (pair): ●x9800
Ceramic brake discs (rotors) rear (pair): ●x8250
Brake pads front for ceramic (pair): ●x535
Brake pads rear for ceramic (pair): ●x535
PSM (ABS) 8.0 hydraulic unit (secondhand): from ●x200
Limited-slip differential: from ●x1120
Front wiper arm assemblies (pair): ●x112
Front wiper blades (pair): ●x45
Rear wiper arm assembly: ●x58
Rear wiper blade: ●x43

Electronic and electrical parts cost
Secondhand PASM control unit: x225
Siemens SDI 3.1 DME (ECU): x5000
PDK transmission control unit: x880
Porsche Communication Management PCM3: from x4699
Window electric motor: x420
Rear wing (spoiler) drive motor: x400
Secondhand rear wing (spoiler) assembly complete with engine lid: from x850
Bosch Alternator: from x476
Lead acid Moll battery: x400
Lithium-ion battery replacement: from x3000

Structural work cost
LHD to RHD conversion: Don't even consider it!
Complete body-in-white restoration: from x15,000
New bodyshell: Price on application from local Porsche dealer
Full repaint (including preparation): from x8000
Full professional restoration from basket case: from x35,000

Manuals
Factory workshop manual set 2009 to 2012: x1.18 per page (official source)
Original 997 owner's (driver's) manual set: x200
PCM3 navigation from x180

Parts that are easy to find
At the time of writing the overwhelming majority of 2nd generation 997 parts are easily sourced from approved Porsche dealers, independent parts suppliers and eBay.

Parts that are hard to find
Porsche ceramic brake discs (rotors) and correct brake pads.
Some control units.
N-rated tyres in some countries.

Parts that are very expensive
The Porsche ceramic brake system (PCCB) is horrendously expensive to maintain.
N-rated tyres in some countries are double the cost of others.

PCCB requires a lot of tender loving care and can be damaged. (Courtesy Porsche AG archive)

3 Living with a 997
– will you get along together?

Purchasing any 911 is going to have an impact on your entire family and, like its ancestors, the 2nd generation 997 is not practical and not really a family car. It was designed for high speed driving through the mountains or hurtling down the Autobahn, Autoroute, Autostrada, Highway, Freeway and Motorways found around the world. However, it is better than its ancestors at sitting in heavy city traffic because it's water-cooled.

Why do you want one of these? (Courtesy Porsche AG archive)

The youngest 997 available in most parts of the world at the time of writing is two years old and the oldest six, and the 997 makes a very good executive daily driver. However, adding the resultant miles and engine operating time will reduce (depreciate) its resale value.

The 997 is a beautiful experience to be enjoyed, but does it genuinely fit into your current lifestyle? Do you have a family? The 997 is a big boys' or girls' toy; a mid-life crisis fun machine designed for two consenting adults to enjoy in the fast lane. The rear seats are totally impractical for an adult, and not suitable for children (author's personal opinion). Porsche baby seats for the 997 are designed and approved to be fitted in the front passenger seat only and require the passenger side airbag system front and side airbags to be disabled.

Are you prepared to look after the 997? As with any thoroughbred, it needs tender loving care, and is not the type of car that can be started and seconds later driven off, parked after a short drive, and the process begun again. Sufficient time has to be given to allow the oil, transmission fluid and coolant to start flowing. VTG turbochargers of the 997 Turbo have to be given time for the bearing water-cooling and oil lubrication systems to function efficiently.

The 997 excels at high speed in the twisty bits. (Courtesy Porsche AG archive)

There are many electronic systems on the 997 that require time to run through self-test routines before it's driven off.

What about exhaust noise? Is it going to impact your family or your neighbours, or attract the attention of local law enforcement? The standard 997 Carrera is quieter than previous series; however, the optional factory sports exhaust system is louder.

What about money? You can afford to purchase a 997, but can you afford to own one? Are you prepared to pay the cost of ensuring the 997 is always in peak roadworthy condition?

Are you prepared to purchase original parts? Are you prepared to pay a little more (not always the case with all tyre brands) to fit Porsche-approved N-rated tyres?

The purchase of any 997 – be it original Porsche or one tuned by an expert tuning company – will impact your lifestyle, your family and your wallet. However, the Porsche experience of the 997 is worth every penny. Any 2nd generation 997 will turn heads, and is Porsche Excellence at its excellent best, but it doesn't come cheap to purchase because it's so new, and it's never cheap to own.

Porsche Excellence: the limited edition Speedster. (Courtesy Porsche AG archive)

4 Relative values
– which model for you?

The first questions that must be asked are all prefixed with: what do I want?

3.6-litre, 3.8-litre or 3.8-litre turbocharged engine? 6-speed manual or 7-speed Porsche Doppelkupplung (PDK) (automatic) transmission? Rear or all-wheel drive? Coupé, Targa or Cabriolet bodystyle? Standard, S, special and/or rare? Simple, powerful, lightweight and fast? Complex, heavier, full of gimmicks and options? Racer or big city driver?

The 2nd generation 997 model range is not as limited as that which it replaced. There were up to 19 different 2nd generation 997 versions available in model years 2010 and 2011. Spoiled for choice really.

The 2nd generation 997 model range consists of:

• Carrera Coupé and Cabriolet bodystyles fitted with a 3.6-litre DFI engine and 6-speed manual or optional 7-speed PDK transmission.

• Carrera 4 Coupé, Cabriolet and Targa 4 bodystyles fitted with a 3.6-litre DFI engine and 6-speed manual or optional 7-speed PDK transmission.

• Carrera S and GTS Coupé and Cabriolet bodystyles fitted with a 3.8-litre DFI engine and 6-speed manual or optional 7-speed PDK transmission.

• Carrera 4S and 4GTS Coupé and Cabriolet and Targa 4S bodystyles fitted with a 3.8-litre DFI engine and 6-speed manual or optional 7-speed PDK transmission.

• Turbo Coupé and Cabriolet bodystyles fitted with a 3.8-litre turbocharged DFI engine and 6-speed manual or optional 7-speed PDK transmission.

Carrera. (Author's collection)

Targa 4 and 4S.
(Courtesy Porsche AG archive)

Carrera GTS Coupé and Cabriolet.
(Courtesy Porsche AG archive)

Carrera 4 GTS Coupé and Cabriolet.
(Courtesy Porsche AG archive)

911 Sport Classic.
(Courtesy
Porsche AG archive)

Speedster.
(Courtesy
Porsche AG archive)

GT3 RS 3.8-litre.
(Courtesy
Porsche AG archive)

GT3 RS 4.0-litre.
(Courtesy Porsche AG archive)

GT2 RS. (Courtesy Porsche AG archive)

• Turbo S Coupé and S Cabriolet bodystyles with a 3.8-litre turbocharged DFI engine and 6-speed manual or optional 7-speed PDK transmission not forgetting the 918 Spyder Coupé and Cabriolet limited editions for Porsche 918 owners only.
• GT3 and GT3 RS with the 3.8-litre dry-sump engine and manual transmission.
• GT2 RS with a turbocharged 3.6-litre dry-sump engine and manual transmission only.
• 911 Sport Classic and Speedster limited editions fitted with an enhanced 3.8-litre DFI engine and manual transmission only.
• Black and China Editions.

   Relative values between models are very complex to calculate, as any accurate comparison must include all variables. Approximate model relative values are calculated using the 2nd generation 997 Carrera S Coupé with PDK transmission as the 100% datum point.

• Carrera Coupé 80%
• Carrera Cabriolet 85%
• Carrera 4 Coupé 90%
• Carrera 4 Cabriolet 95%
• Targa 4 100%
• Black Edition 100%
• Carrera GTS Coupé 120%
• Carrera S (GTS) Cabriolet 130% (150%)
• Carrera 4S (4GTS) Coupé 140% (160%)
• Carrera 4S (4GTS) Cabriolet 160% (180%)

• Targa 4S 140%
• Sport Classic 200%
• Speedster 250%
• Turbo (S) Coupé 210%
• Turbo (S) Cabriolet 240%
• GT3 (RS) 300%
• GT2 RS 400%

5 Before you view

– be well informed

The key to a successful purchase is research! To avoid a wasted journey it will help if you're very clear about what questions you want to ask before you pick up the telephone. Some of these points might appear basic but when you're excited about the prospect of buying your dream classic, it's amazing how some of the most obvious things slip the mind. Also check the current values of the model you are interested in car magazines, which provide price guides and even auction results.

Where is the car?

Is it going to be worth travelling to the next county, state or to another country? A locally advertised car, although it may not sound very interesting, can add to your knowledge for very little effort, so make a visit – it might even be in better condition than expected.

Dealer or private sale?

Establish early on if the car is being sold by its owner or by a trader. A private owner should have all the history, so don't be afraid to ask detailed questions. A dealer may have more limited knowledge of a car's history, but should have some documentation. A dealer may offer a warranty/guarantee (ask for a printed copy) and finance. Private sales = no warranty and all legal liability on the purchasers shoulders.

Cost of collection and delivery?

A dealer will be used to quoting for delivery using car transporters. A private owner may agree to meet you halfway, but only do so after you have seen the car at the vendor's address to validate the documents. Conversely, you could meet halfway and agree the sale but insist on meeting at the vendor's address for the handover.

View – when and where?

It is always preferable to view at the vendor's home or business premises. In the case of a private sale, the car's documentation must tally with the vendor's name and address. Arrange to view only in daylight and avoid wet days. Most cars look better in poor light or when wet.

Reason for sale

Do make it one of the first questions. Why is the car being sold and how long has it been with the current owner? How many previous owners?

Left-hand drive to right-hand drive

Porsche manufactured its model range to comply with individual national requirements. There are nations with right-hand drive regulations that allow local registration of left-hand drive cars, but if left-hand drive is not permitted and private right-hand drive imports restricted or banned then a third party conversion may be your only choice, but explore all other avenues first.

Condition (body/chassis/interior/mechanicals)

Ask for an honest appraisal of the car's condition. Ask specifically about some of the check items described in Chapter 7. A full systems check and test drive is mandatory.

All original specification

A completely original 997's value is invariably higher than one with aftermarket modifications except the professionally tuned versions. Think of the standard market price for the model and start by doubling it to get into the basic ballpark.

Matching data/legal ownership

It's mandatory for any potential purchaser to ensure the VIN, engine serial number and licence plate (if applicable) matches the official registration documentation? Is the owner's name and address recorded in the official registration documents?

For those countries that require roadworthiness inspections such as an MoT certificate in the UK or Fahrtzeugausweis in Germany and Switzerland, does the car have a document showing it complies? If an exhaust and/or noise emissions certificate is mandatory, does the car have one? Does the car have current road tax or equivalent as required in numerous countries such as the UK and Germany? Does the vendor own the car outright? Money might be owed to a finance company or bank: the car could even be stolen. Many nations have government or private organisations that will supply accurate and complete vehicle ownership data, based on the car's licence plate number and/or VIN, for a fee. These organisations can often also provide information related to the car's accident history such as: has the car previously been declared 'written-off' by an insurance company after an accident. In the UK the following organisations can supply vehicle data:

HPI	0113 222 2010	AA	0113 222 2010
DVLA	0844 453 0118	RAC	0330 159 0364

Unleaded fuel

All 997s were designed to run on unleaded fuel only.

Insurance

Check with your existing insurer before setting out, your current policy or that of the vendor may not cover you to drive the car if you do purchase it. Do not drive uninsured cars and, if in doubt, always ask.

How you can pay

A cheque/check will take several days to clear and the seller may prefer to sell to a cash buyer. However, a banker's draft (a cheque issued by a bank) is as good as cash, but safer, so contact your own bank and become familiar with the formalities that are necessary to obtain one.

Buying at auction?

If the intention is to buy at auction, see Chapter 10 for further advice.

Professional vehicle check (mechanical examination)

There are often marque/model specialists who will undertake professional examination of a vehicle on your behalf. Porsche clubs will be able to put you in touch with specialists. Porsche dealerships offer similar services.

6 Inspection equipment
– these items will really help

Before you rush out of the door, gather together a few items that will help as you undertake a more thorough inspection.

This book
This book is designed to be your guide at every step, so take it along and use the check boxes to help you assess each area of the car you're interested in. Don't be afraid to let the seller see you using it. Take the author's other books with you, if you have them.

Reading glasses (if you need them for close work)
Take your reading glasses, if you need them to read documents and make close up inspections. The author has to take his off for close-up work, so carry a glasses case if you have to do the same.

Magnet (not powerful, a fridge magnet is ideal)
A magnet will help you check if the car is full of filler, or has fibreglass or carbon-fibre panels. Ask the seller's permission first before using a magnet. Some may prefer you to use a paint depth meter. If permission is granted, use the magnet to sample bodywork areas all around the car, but be careful not to damage the paintwork.

Torch (flashlight)
A torch with fresh batteries will be useful for peering into the front spoiler to check radiator condition, but remember the 997 has many panels covering up entire areas.

Probe (a small screwdriver works very well)
A small screwdriver can be used – with care – as a probe, particularly in the wheelarches and on the underside. However, 997s suffering from structural corrosion are extremely rare, so be careful what you start probing, and always ask the seller's permission before probing their car.

Overalls
Be prepared to get dirty. Take along a pair of overalls, if you have them.

Mirror on a stick
Fixing a mirror at an angle on the end of a stick may seem odd, but you'll probably need it to check the condition of the underside of the car. It will also help you to peer into some of the important crevices. You can also use it, together with the torch, along the underside of the sills and on the floor. Remember that a completely original 997 is panelled the entire length of its underside.

Digital camera
This is a mandatory piece of inspection equipment. If you don't have a digital camera, use your mobile phone. Take lots of pictures of all parts of the car whether they cause you concern or not. When you get home study them, seek an expert's

opinion. Sometimes photographs viewed in the quiet of your own home will reveal things you missed in the heat of the moment.

A friend; preferably a knowledgeable enthusiast

Ideally, have a friend or knowledgeable enthusiast accompany you: a second opinion is always valuable and also provides a level of personal security.

www.velocebooks.com / www.veloce.co.uk
Details of all current books • New book news • Special offers • Gift vouchers • Forum

17

7 Fifteen minute evaluation
– walk away or stay?

Exterior

Ensuring the 997 is parked on level ground, begin the exterior inspection by looking for obvious signs of body damage and accident repairs.

Check the panel gaps.
(Courtesy Callas Rennsport)

Walk around the 997, randomly carefully placing the magnet on areas of the bodywork. If it sticks move on; if not, find out why.

Corrosion (rust) damage is easy to spot, as the paint will be bubbled and/or cracked. Randomly measure the body panel gaps, around luggage compartment lid, engine lid and doors. If the gaps are even, it usually means the body is straight. Any inconsistencies in gap measurements indicate that the 997 has undergone major accident repairs.

Look for obvious signs of repainting, such as different shades, and overspray.

Porsche painting is of the highest quality. The best place to look for overspray is in hard-to-get-at places, such as forward of the doors or under the wheel wells. A poor repaint is immediate grounds to walk away. A good quality repaint should not deter you from purchasing, but allow renegotiation of the price – down! Check for minor front or rear end collisions by inspecting bumper bars for cracks and splits in the plastic.

Check around the front light assemblies for stone chip damage and cracked lenses. With the torch blazing, check the condition of the front of the radiators through the front spoiler. The standard number of radiators installed is two for all Carrera and Carrera S models (RWD and AWD), and three for the Turbo, GT3, GT3 RS, GT2 RS models, options X51 and i183 (super hot climate). Reach into the radiator area (only when cold), and check for debris. The excellent aerodynamic design, which draws cooling air into the radiator cores, also acts as a powerful vacuum cleaner, sucking up almost anything that passes in front of the 997.

Check the condition of the rear light assemblies.

Check all seals. 997 door windows close into a body-mounted seal, as the door has no upper frame.

Ensure the seller extends the rear wing (spoiler), if installed, to its fully open position to permit access. Inspect the rear wing (spoiler) assembly for any evidence of corrosion in the mechanism. Apart from the 911 Sport Classic, GT3, RS, RS 4.0-litre and GT2 RS models, all other 2nd generation 997 models are fitted with an extend and retract rear wing (spoiler) system of two different designs: the normally-aspirated engine and turbocharged engine version.

997 Carrera model rear wing
(spoiler) extended. (Courtesy
Porsche AG archive)

Check the condition of the sealing curtain fitted inside the normally-aspirated engine rear wing (spoiler) system for condition: torn or missing is not good. Get the seller to retract the rear wing (spoiler) to its fully closed or stowed position. Whilst checking the exterior, inspect the brake discs (rotors), callipers and pads. Pad thickness must be greater than 2mm (0.08in) and the discs (rotors) must not be damaged. Replacing brake discs (rotors) and pads is very expensive. If fitted with Porsche ceramic brake discs (rotors), check for physical damage to the edges caused by wheel removal and re-installation. Check for evidence of brake fluid leakage over any components in the wheel wells, including the rear of each wheel.

Check condition of suspension in the wheel wells.

If looking at a Cabriolet model, ask the seller to raise the hydraulic-powered roof and properly inspect the fabric, as it's very expensive to replace. Check sealing and condition of the glass window, as well as condition and alignment of the frame, with the roof open and closed. It's critically important that the seller open and close a cabriolet roof so you can see it in operation, and don't forget to ask about any repairs to the roof system since delivery. Check for hydraulic leaks in the Cabriolet storage area, and ensure, if there's a hardtop present, that it's painted in the same colour as the exterior. With the 997 series not every Cabriolet was delivered with a matching hardtop as it was only offered as an option costing around $US3460.

If the 997 under inspection is a Targa 4 bodystyle, ensure the entire panoramic glass roof module – including the glass roof, roller blind and rear glass hatch – are opened, and that all areas including water drains, roof structural components, fabric and lining condition are inspected. Close everything and ensure the interior roller blind functions correctly also.

When doing an exterior inspection, always check the ground around the car for any evidence of leaks: oil, coolant, transmission oil and washer systems water.

Turbocharged rear wing (spoiler) extended. (Courtesy Porsche AG archive)

Check the fixed rear wing (spoiler) if it's a GT model. (Courtesy Porsche AG archive)

Check Cabriolet roof operation. (Author's collection)

Interior

Inspect all interior fittings and assemblies, including a full inspection of each seat for condition, ensuring none of the main or trim materials is cracked, torn, faded or missing. A cracked dash is extremely expensive to repair. Lower the rear seat backs and check behind. Inspect the instruments for any damage or fading. Ensure the internal lighting system works.

Check all electric seat functions. If a set of controls is not working, it's possible that those functions were not installed at the factory, but check the options list. The

An engine bay
inspection is mandatory.
(Courtesy Porsche AG archive)

driver's seat motor drive connector is easily damaged and can cause all kinds of issues, not just with trying to move the seat. If seat heating is installed, check this as well. These items are often overlooked and are expensive to repair.

Ask the seller if there have been any problems with the airbags, if installed. Some owners disconnect the passenger airbag so children can occupy the front seat. If disabled, ensure that it's correctly labelled.

Check that all the combined interior light and switch assemblies operate correctly, and inspect the light assemblies, which vary in location and design between models.

Check for moisture in the carpets and, if possible, check the condition of the control units installed under both seats, which vary depending on model.

Run the electric windows down and back up to see if there's any moisture trapped in the door. Empty the contents of each door pocket and check for moisture. A good tip is to wipe the inside of each pocket with a tissue (Kleenex) and see if it picks up anything. Empty the contents of the glove box (if installed) and check for evidence of moisture, damage to switches and cables. Does the light come on? And check if there's an owners manual somewhere in the car.

Compartments and mechanicals
In the 2nd generation 997 series, the luggage compartment and engine lids are electrically operated by buttons installed in the driver's side door sill, which is a brilliant system unless the battery goes flat.

Open the luggage compartment lid and ensure the gas struts hold it up. Inspect the seal, which runs around the body, for condition and any evidence of moisture. Make sure the emergency lid release cable is present. The 997 series luggage compartment is fully panelled inside (panelling and trim shape and coverage varies with option status), and inspecting some items beneath the panelling is not easy, but it can be done with the owner's agreement. Remove the plastic battery cover in the centre rear of the compartment and inspect the battery for condition, and any evidence of acid spill and/or corrosion.

Check the compartment panelled areas for moisture damage and staining. If everything is clean, what lies beneath is probably in good condition.

Open up the tool kit and check that all tools are present and not damaged or rusted. Ensure the spare-tyre-in-a-tin (sealant) is present, along with an air-compressor and tyre pressure gauge.

Open the engine lid and ensure the gas strut holds it open. Check for rub marks on the edges of the engine lid and on the bodywork. Look for signs of structural repair. Make sure the emergency lid release cable is present. Check the condition of the engine and components,

Inspect the luggage compartment.
(Author's collection)

looking for obvious signs of oil, coolant and power steering fluid leakage. 997 water-cooled engines have no distributor or conventional sparkplug wires.

Check for obvious engine modifications, such as a K&N air filter assembly installation. Inspecting turbocharged engines is much more difficult due to additional installations in the engine bay, such as the intercoolers. However the 997 is not fitted with a rear engine cover, so access from underneath is much easier than previous 911 series.

Is it genuine and legal?

Ask the seller for all documentation related to the car, including owner's manual, service record book, emissions inspection reports, any import documentation, roadworthiness inspection certificates, and all repair receipts. Only buy a Porsche from an individual who can prove that they are the person named in the car's registration document (V5C in the UK) and, preferably, at the address shown in the document. Also check that the VIN or chassis number and engine numbers of the car match the numbers in the registration document.

Check the service record book: is it the original, or a replacement (duplicate)? A duplicate record book will have 'duplicate' stamped on each page.

The traditional white label under the luggage compartment lid may not be present on the 997, due to change in labelling policy at the factory. Two labels were put in the glove compartment for the dealer to put in place, and many didn't. The label may be under the lid, there may be a copy in the service record book, there may not be on both counts. On most 997s inspected by the author, there's at least one label present, but not on all. When identifying any 911, the most important number to find is the vehicle identification number (VIN): 17 digits, of which the 10th digit indicates the model year. If the label is present, it also contains the 997 model

type code, engine type, engine code, transmission type, paint code, interior colour combination code, country code and basic options list. If this label is missing, ask the seller why? With the 997, it's possible the seller cannot answer why the label(s) are missing, but they must provide other original documentation, such as the delivery papers. If there's no original paperwork with provenance, walk away.

If the label is present, the VIN on it must match the VINs found at numerous locations in the car, such as behind the windscreen (windshield), and in the luggage compartment rear right and right lower side (both accessed under panelling). VINs must also match national registration and insurance documentation.

A proper authenticity check also includes physically inspecting the engine serial number (engraved on a boss on the crankcase lower rear left), checking its date of manufacture (plate found in luggage compartment right lower side), and ensuring that these numbers match the type and codes on the identification label and other paperwork. The engine serial number must match all registration documentation. Confirm the 997's paint code. Match the paint code found on the identification label, if it's present, with the label on the rear driver's side door jamb and delivery papers.

Ask the seller

There are some things that only the most experienced 997 expert is going to find during a 15-minute inspection. For the first time buyer, it's much better to go armed with these important questions:

• Was this 997 originally built for the market (country) it's being sold in?
• Has this car been tracked or used in any form of motorsport?
• Is the mileage genuine?
• Is the car a weekend warrior or was it used as a daily driver?
• Was it regularly driven in heavy traffic?
• Has the car been involved in an accident?
• Has the engine and/or transmission been repaired or modified?
• Have the rubber hoses and belts been replaced?
• If it's a 997 Cabriolet, was there a hardtop?
• Are there any known problems with any of the car's electrical or electronic systems?

Common sense has to prevail, with the buyer weighing up whether they are being told the truth or not. If you purchase a 997 with problems, it can be extremely frustrating to repair. As the model range expanded, so did the complexity. Porsche offered the 2nd generation 997 Carrera models in a standard basic form with a 3.6-litre DFI engine, but without bells and whistles. It also offered a more powerful and complicated S model range, with all the bells and whistles and even more options, and an enhanced 3.8-litre DFI engine for some of the later GTS models, and many of the limited editions.

Restoration of a basket case

There are very few 997 basket cases available. It's not worth purchasing a 997 wreck, unless there's a specific requirement, such as going racing, and this essentially means picking up an accident-damaged GT3 or GT3 RS model. Good luck with that. Restoration of any of the other 2nd generation 997 series is not an economic option – unless the purchase price is very low, and you are a masochist.

8 Key points
– where to look for problems

Pay particular attention to these, and understand what you are looking at!

Get up close and personal.
(Author's collection)

Radiators in a Carrera are behind the
left and right sides of the front apron.
(Author's collection)

Targa's glass roof and rear hatch must be opened and inspected.
(Courtesy Porsche AG archive)

Inspect the front light modules.
(Author's collection)

Are the wheels approved? And
inspect what's behind the spokes.
(Author's collection)

The rear wing (spoiler) sealing curtain is relatively inexpensive to replace. (Courtesy Porsche AG archive)

The identification label is very important. (Author's collection)

Check the door sill luggage compartment and engine lid release system. (Author's collection)

Carrera 3.6-litre MA1.02 engine. (Courtesy Porsche AG archive)

Carrera S 3.8-litre MA1.01 engine. (Courtesy Porsche AG archive)

www.velocebooks.com / www.veloce.co.uk
Details of all current books • New book news • Special offers • Gift vouchers • Forum

24

9 Serious evaluation
– 60 minutes for years of enjoyment

Circle Excellent (4), Good (3), Average (2) or Poor (1) for each check, and add up points at the end. Any evaluation check must be realistic. Sole responsibility lies with the buyer to be vigilant and not cut corners over the next 60 minutes. Take it seriously, get it right, and you will be able to make an informed decision on whether to purchase. Get it wrong, and it could become your worst nightmare.

How does it look just sitting there?

The 997 is a thoroughbred sports car manufactured for high-performance motoring. It is not a toy and, if not set up properly, it will bite its owner. Before starting any evaluation ensure the 997 is sitting on level ground. Does it sit level? Look at it from all angles. Is it clean inside and out? Does it look smart, or a little tired? Does it smell of fast food? Does it look original? What's your first impression? This evaluation check is based on first impressions.

First impressions count. (Courtesy Porsche AG archive)

What about the interior and
exterior colour combination?
(Courtesy Porsche AG archive)

Exterior and interior colour combination ④ ③ ② ①

Everybody thinks at sometime about the resale value of his or her car. One huge value killer can be the exterior and interior colour combination. Men can be very practical on this subject and say: "I could get used to it or I can learn to live with it." Get your partner's opinion, *then* rate it.

Exterior paint ④ ③ ② ①

When inspecting a car's paintwork, remember the old saying 'you can always replace the mechanicals, but you can never replace the body.' The 997 is difficult to repair properly, especially structurally, and the Porsche workshop manual repair schemes are complicated, requiring specialist equipment. In reality, there are two types of paintwork repairs that are carried out: the 'sell on immediately' repair (and

pass the problem on to a new owner); or the 'keep the car' repair – this form of repair is naturally more desirable to any buyer, but only if carried out by an experienced professional who won't cut corners. This is why an inspection and assessment of the paintwork is so critical. Paintwork is covered in Chapter 7 but, if you have any doubts, take as much time as you like before making an assessment decision. Rust is not a major issue in the 997, but poor accident damage repairs have been identified within the 997 community, and rust could develop in the repaired areas. Rating is for condition.

Get up close
and personal
with the paint.
(Author's collection)

Body panel condition (including door bases) ④ ③ ② ①

Battle damage from debris on the road is a fact of life. A normal unmodified 997 sits significantly lower than other standard road cars and is always in the firing line. If the 997 is completely clean, without any evidence of stone chips, this indicates that it hasn't been driven, or has recently been repaired, and/or completely repainted.

Body panel damage, such as small dents and scrapes, should be assessed during the inspection. Scratches around the door locks and handles are normal, but the question for the buyer is: can visible damage be repaired using the latest minor dent removal technologies, or is more serious and costly repair required?

Walk around the 997 with a ruler and measure the gaps between all moving panels and surrounding metalwork, which should all be even. Don't forget to compare one side with the other. Rating in this area is for irregularities in gap measurements and visible damage, no matter how small or seemingly insignificant.

Inspect the underside structure of the luggage
compartment lid. (Author's collection)

Seals   ④ ③ ② ①

Check the condition of all visible rubber seals, especially those around the front and rear glass, door frame and luggage compartment and engine lid. Seal damage means water can get in. Rating is for condition and replacement cost if damaged.

Radiators and coolant   ④ ③ ② ①

Radiator condition can only be assessed by a visual inspection of what can be seen through the front apron. Air-conditioning condenser-mixers are mounted in front of each radiator, so it's the condenser-mixers that are really being inspected. If these are in good condition, the actual coolant radiators behind should be in good condition too. If you wish to have full access to the radiators for a detailed inspection, the front section underside panel and bumper bar have to be removed. Every 997 has two coolant radiators (with a condenser-mixer mounted in front), with an additional centre front radiator fitted to the Turbo model range, all GT models and options X51 and i183 (super hot climate).

All 997 models are fitted with heat exchangers used for engine oil cooling, using coolant as the cooling agent. Transmission fluid cooling, using a coolant heat exchanger, is also fitted to the GT model manual transmissions and the optional 7-speed PDK transmission). It's not possible to determine the interior condition of the heat exchangers or condition of the front radiators by visual inspection; however, a quick check of the coolant colour in the overflow/filling container in the engine bay will provide vital clues. Original coolant colour will be dependent on local products used, but if the coolant has mixed with oil, or with transmission fluid in the engine, transmission or heat exchanger, it will be muddy brown. If the current owner has not used the proper coolant/anti-freeze mixture, and used water instead, the overflow container contents will also be muddy brown in colour. Contaminated coolant is a reason to stop the inspection and walk away. Rating is for radiator/condenser-mixer assembly condition and coolant colour.

Lights   ④ ③ ② ①

Check the condition of all light assembly lenses, and operation of all installed lighting systems, front and rear, including indicator, brake and foglights. A 997 with an engine lid installed rear wing (spoiler) has two brakelight assemblies built into the engine lid, with one visible when the rear wing (spoiler) is closed, and the other when it's fully extended. Rating is for all installed light assembly condition and correct operation.

The condition of all compartment seals is important. (Author's collection)

Radiator access from the front is limited. (Author's collection)

Check the ducting in the centre lower front apron. (Author's collection)

Check the coolant colour. (Author's collection)

Front wipers and the washer system must be closely inspected. (Author's collection)

Headlight washer nozzles, if installed, must also be inspected. (Author's collection)

Wipers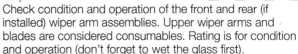

Check condition and operation of the front and rear (if installed) wiper arm assemblies. Upper wiper arms and blades are considered consumables. Rating is for condition and operation (don't forget to wet the glass first).

Washers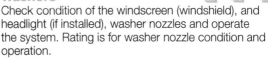

Check condition of the windscreen (windshield), and headlight (if installed), washer nozzles and operate the system. Rating is for washer nozzle condition and operation.

Cabriolet rag and hardtop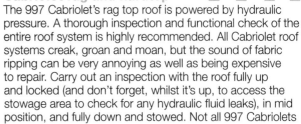

The 997 Cabriolet's rag top roof is powered by hydraulic pressure. A thorough inspection and functional check of the entire roof system is highly recommended. All Cabriolet roof systems creak, groan and moan, but the sound of fabric ripping can be very annoying as well as being expensive to repair. Carry out an inspection with the roof fully up and locked (and don't forget, whilst it's up, to access the stowage area to check for any hydraulic fluid leaks), in mid position, and fully down and stowed. Not all 997 Cabriolets were delivered with hardtops; if there is a hardtop included in the sale, it must be painted in the same colour as the 997's exterior. A bad roof is a deal breaker. Rating is for rag top fabric, frame, window and seal condition, hardtop condition (if included in sale), and roof operational check.

Check the Cabriolet roof in various positions. (Courtesy Porsche AG archive)

Check around the cover compartment with the roof closed ... (Courtesy Porsche AG archive)

... and open ... (Courtesy Porsche AG archive)

... and, if it's a Speedster, its mechanical roof must be checked. (Courtesy Porsche AG archive)

Don't forget the hardtop, if included in the sale. (Courtesy Porsche AG archive)

Targa roof and rear hatch

The 997 Targa roof module consists of a glass sunroof, wind deflector, sun-blind, rear folding window (opening hatchback) and all associated system components. A full inspection with the roof open and closed, and the rear folding window open and closed, is strongly recommended, including checking all seals, water drains and the roof structure, for signs of paint bubbling and other forms of corrosion or damage. Rating is for condition, correct operation of all components, drain, paint and structural condition, evidence of water ingress and noise levels (test drive).

Inspect the complete Targa glass roof module ... (Courtesy Porsche AG archive)

... from all angles ...
(Courtesy Porsche AG archive)

... and don't forget the rear glass hatch.
(Courtesy Porsche AG archive)

If installed, ask the seller to operate the sunroof …
(Author's collection)

… to its fully open position …
(Author's collection)

… and fully closed.
(Author's collection)

997 Carrera standard 18in wheels.
(Author's collection)

Sunroof

4 3 2 1

If it's a Coupé with a sunroof and lots do, ask for it to be opened, closed, lifted and tilted. Ensure the wind deflector is deployed once the roof panel is fully retracted. Inspect the roof panel seals, and for any evidence of water ingress and rust. Ask the seller to close the sunroof, and watch the panel operation as it slides forward. Rating is for condition and operation.

Glass

4 3 2 1

Before carrying out a vehicle inspection, find out what rules apply regarding glass damage. Is a single chip or crack sufficient to fail a roadworthiness inspection? Rate glass condition on how it impacts roadworthiness.

Wheels

4 3 2 1

Check the wheels are correct for the model being inspected, by comparing what's physically installed with the owner's manual. Incorrect wheels can cause serious problems, including wheel rub and unsafe handling. This inspection relates to safety as well as roadworthiness. If there's any doubt, ask the seller for additional paperwork on the wheels. Condition of each wheel is critically important, as corrosion can lead to fatigue cracking and structural failure. Genuine Porsche factory wheels five-bolt and centre-lock, even if painted, are clear coated; if this coating is peeling, it will be costly to get it repaired. Inspect for impact damage around the rim. Look at the relationship between the wheels and the wheelarch. On a standard 997, the wheels should be inline with the wheelarch, but if the wheels are noticeably angled in at the top, that means that the current owner has a lot of camber dialled in. Rating is for wheel originality and condition.

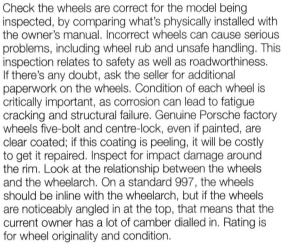

What rating should this 18in wheel's condition receive?
(Author's collection)

Wheel well linings 4 3 2 1

Ensure all are fitted; check condition of the plastic and mounting screws. Rating is for condition.

Wheel bearings and 4 3 2 1
half-shafts

997 wheel bearings are almost bullet proof and rarely fail. In the 997 series, the wheel bearing forms part of the wheel speed sensor system, making condition more important. If something is screaming like a banshee whilst driving, it's more likely that it's the CV joint of the halfshaft. However, to check the wheel bearings, remove the wheel centre cap (if it's possible) and, using a torch (flashlight), inspect for evidence of metal filings and overheating. A failed wheel bearing will get very hot, will blue the cotter pin, and burn the lubricating grease within the bearing and deposit soot around the wheel bearing housing. If metal debris or evidence of overheating is discovered, jack the affected wheel off the ground and rotate it. If grinding scrapping noises are heard, it's likely either the wheel bearing and/or the halfshaft CV joint has failed. However, the test drive will reveal any rotating part with failed bearing surfaces, because it will scream like a banshee. Locating the source of the noise, however, will require a thorough inspection. Rating is for condition of the wheel bearing and whether a further more detailed inspection is warranted.

Tyre condition, suitability 4 3 2 1
and wheel alignment

Who owns a thoroughbred sports car capable of speeds in excess of 280kph (174mph) and installs cheap tyres or mixes and matches tyre brands from side to side and front to rear in order to save money? Those four black round bits of rubber wrapped around the wheels are the only things holding the 997 on the road. Why spend huge amount of money purchasing a precision high-performance sports car, and then put everyone at risk by installing cheap useless tyres? A set of approved and tested tyres for the 997 not only gives it the ability to perform at its maximum in the handling department, it also allows the maximum transfer of power to the road and ensures the braking system provides maximum stopping power at all times. The 997 is designed to be driven on approved summer tyres in summer and the correct winter tyres in winter. It was not designed around all-season el-cheapo jack-of-all trade tyres. Don't drive a 997 on summer tyres when the road temperature drops below 7°C (45°F), switch to winter tyres. Why?

Underneath with the digital camera to check the engine serial number. (Author's collection)

Only a test drive is going to reveal wheel bearing issues. (Courtesy Porsche AG archive)

See Chapter 17 for the approved tyres list. (Courtesy Paul Simmons)

Centre-lock wheels were introduced for some 2nd generation 997 models. (Courtesy Joe Ramos)

Winter tyres are made from a softer compound, heat up more quickly and don't go hard. To give just one example: if the road is wet and is at a temperature of 7°C (45°F), summer tyres will require 38% more braking distance from 80kph (50mph) to a full stop compared to winter tyres. Check tyres for: same brand, same tread pattern, correct size front and rear for the installed wheels and in accordance with the owner's manual. See the table in Chapter 17. It contains an up-to-date list of all tyres approved and tested by Porsche for the 997 series. Look at the wear across each tyre. Is it even? Is there more on the outside than inside or vice versa? A bad wheel alignment will cause tyres to wear unevenly. Rating is for tyre condition (bubbles and cracks), uneven wear, age (more than six years old), suitability and cost of a wheel alignment if required.

Steering system

All 997 models are fitted with a power assisted rack and pinion steering. The power steering system requires the engine to be running. Any grinding and air cavitation noises from the engine mounted power steering pump will be obvious. With the engine still running, turn the steering wheel full left and then full right, listening for any unusual sounds.

Check under the front for fluid leakage. This may not be immediately obvious, so slide some butcher's paper (described later under oil leaks) under the front and under the right side of the engine and come back later to check. Rating is for system component inspection and condition, static test with engine running and any detected fluid leaks.

Standard 2nd generation 997 Carrera 4-piston brake calliper. (Author's collection)

Red brake calliper and centre-lock wheel of the Carrera GTS. (Courtesy Joe Ramos)

Standard red 997 Turbo brake calliper. (Courtesy Porsche AG archive)

997 Turbo S with full PCCB brake system. (Courtesy Porsche AG archive)

Brake callipers and pads ④ ③ ② ①

A basic brake calliper inspection can be carried out by looking through the wheels, but it's better to have the wheel turned full left and then full right to allow better access to the callipers and to be able to view the brake pads. Brake callipers come in different colours depending on the model (black, red and yellow). See Chapter 17 for more information. Inspect the brake pads: the lining should be more than 2mm thick. Pads must be changed at 2mm to ensure the warning detectors are not activated because, if they are, they have to be replaced as well. Rating is for calliper condition as well thickness of the brake pad lining, which may need replacement – creating a near future cost issue.

Brake discs (rotors) ④ ③ ② ①

Most 2nd generation 997s were delivered standard with perforated (cross-drilled holes) and ventilated front and rear brake discs (rotors) manufactured from grey cast iron (aka steel). The GT2 RS, GT3 RS and later 2nd generation models and limited editions, were fitted with PCCB ceramic brake discs (rotors) as standard. To determine originality, consult the owner manual. Check steel brake disc (rotor) wear, looking for cracks between the holes, blocked holes, or grooves cut into the disc (rotor). Consideration has to be given to overall brake disc thickness which, during such an evaluation, is hard to check. Look at each disc (rotor) carefully. Is there a lip or edge cut around the outer circumference? Such a lip indicates that the brake pads have worn away both faces of the brake disc (rotor), and at the next service all will have to be replaced. If ceramic brake discs (rotors) are installed, pay particular attention for cracks and damage at the edge. Ceramic discs (rotors) are easily damaged by actions such as wheel removal and installation. Rating is for brake disc (rotor) originality, condition and wear.

Handbrake (emergency or park brake) ④ ③ ② ①

The handbrake (emergency or park brake) must be tested to ensure it holds the 997 under all circumstances. Rating is for the handbrake (emergency or park brake) holding ability.

Rear wing (spoiler) ④ ③ ② ①

Apart from the GT models and the 911 Sport Classic all 2nd generation 997s were delivered with an electro-mechanical extend and retract rear wing (spoiler) system. There are two designs of rear wing (spoiler), a vertical moving assembly fitted to the

Rear wing (spoiler) integrated in the engine lid. (Courtesy Porsche AG archive)

Rear wing (spoiler) extended. Check the sealing curtain and the fourth brakelight. (Courtesy Porsche AG archive)

turbocharged 997 models and the integrated wing (spoiler) installed into the engine lid on all normally-aspirated 997 models. Regardless of which type is installed, ask the seller to extend it. Check that the mechanism does not bind or jam when moving. Once the rear wing (spoiler) is fully extended, check the condition of the sealing curtain. Also with the integrated engine lid rear wing (spoiler), check the fourth brakelight fitted to the rear wing (spoiler). It's only visible when it's extended. It comes on when the brake pedal is pressed. Ask the seller to retract the rear wing (spoiler), ensuring it retracts correctly and is stowed evenly. Rating is for rear wing (spoiler) condition and electro-mechanical operation.

Engine bay top inspection   4   3   2   1

The engine lid latch is released using the switch mounted on the driver's side doorsill. Lift the lid to its full open position and ensure the gas strut holds it open. Don't forget there are differences in engine size dependent on model. Standard 997 Carrera models have a 3.6-litre and the S models have a 3.8-litre DFI engine. 2nd generation turbocharged models all have 3.8-litre DFI engines except for the GT2 RS, which retains its dry-sump 3.6-litre turbocharged engine. The GT3 is fitted with a dry-sump 3.8-litre engine, and derivatives of the same engine type are installed in the GT3 RS and GT 3 RS 4.0-litre. Inspect all visible components

Carrera 4 GTS engine bay.
(Courtesy Porsche AG archive)

911 Sport Classic engine bay.
(Courtesy Porsche AG archive)

Turbo S engine bay.
(Courtesy Porsche AG archive)

Inspect the left and right rear
hydraulic engine mounts.
(Author's collection)

Inspect the purge fan
and its fittings on the
underside of the engine
lid. (Author's collection)

in the engine bay. Each engine type has only a single polyrib belt driving all of its accessories, so the belt's condition is very important. Corrosion on the engine and associated components is quite common, if the 997 has been driven in winter. Check for any visible signs of engine modification, in particular the air-filter assembly. If anything causes alarm, ask the seller about it. Rating is for condition of all visible components, component originality, all visible metalwork, and engine bay cleanliness.

Fuel filler cap, cover and luggage compartment

The fuel cap cover over the fuel filler cap located on the right side fender (guard/wing) can be opened by hand any time the doors are unlocked. Check the condition of the fuel cap cover, and ensure the required labels are installed on its underside. Labels vary with national requirements. Check condition of fuel filler cap. Check the fuel cap cover is locked when the doors are locked.

The luggage compartment lid safety latch is unlocked using a switch mounted on the driver's side doorsill. The safety catch has to be physically released using the red lever under the popped lid. Lift the luggage compartment lid to its fully open position and ensure the gas struts hold it open. Check condition of all carpets and panelling. Components such as the fuel tank are not easily accessed. The battery cover can be removed, and the battery and surrounds inspected. Check that the safety triangle is present, and also the first-aid kit. Some nations require other emergency equipment, such as safety vests. Open up the tool kit and check all the tools. Check the spare-tyre-in-a-tin is present (tyre sealant), as no 997 (outside four known nations in the Middle East) is fitted with a spare tyre. Rating is for the condition of all components that can be inspected, luggage compartment condition, and the presence and condition of all required accessories, tools and emergency equipment.

Battery charging rate

With the engine running at idle, connect a digital multi meter across the battery terminals: the voltage shown on the display must be between 13.8 and 14.2VDC. To check

Open the fuel filler cap cover and check for correct labelling. (Author's collection)

Right-hand drive 2nd generation Carrera luggage compartment. (Author's collection)

The battery is easily exposed in any 2nd generation 997. (Courtesy Joe Ramos)

Left-hand drive Carrera GTS luggage compartment. (Courtesy Joe Ramos)

battery condition, turn the engine off and measure the voltage between the terminals again: it should be between 12.4 and 12.6VDC. Rating is a pass or fail – either all good, or bad because repairs are required.

Tow hook [4] [3] [2] [1]

The tow hook can be installed into a threaded section of the 997's body structure accessed through the front or rear bumper bar via holes covered with a small, easily

The tow hook is part of the tool kit in a 997. (Courtesy Joe Ramos)

removed plastic cover. A quick check to ensure the 997 unibody (combined chassis and boy structure) is straight is to insert the tow hook. If the tow hook starts to resist and twists at an angle or cannot even be inserted straight this is a definite sign of an accident-damaged and bent unibody. Rating is a pass with deductions for tow hook, bumper bar hole and cover condition. Walk away, if the 997 fails this test.

Interior water ingress check [4] [3] [2] [1]

Open the doors and check along the bottom of each door for any evidence of water. Run the electric windows down and up to see if the window picks up any moisture. Open each of the door storage compartments, checking for obvious signs of dampness or water-damaged contents. Dab a Kleenex tissue around any suspect areas inside, including the carpets, to see if it picks up any moisture. Rating should reflect how much, if any, moisture was discovered.

Interior [4] [3] [2] [1]

The interior inspection is all about originality of installed seats, seat belts dash, carpet, mats and trim. Inspect for rips, tears, staining, mould, repairs, fraying seat belts, whether the seatbelt lower stitched loop still intact (if it's been in an accident, the loop will be broken on impact), seatbelt inertial reels front and rear, and any other forms of damage. Check all the interior lights function when the doors are opened (on) and closed (off). Check the condition of the roof liner. Check all electrical and mechanical functions of the driver and passenger seats in accordance

Interior: condition, condition, condition – and originality! (Courtesy Joe Ramos)

GT3 RS 4.0-litre racing bucket seats. (Courtesy Porsche AG archive)

with the owner's manual. Check that the rear seat backs can be released, lowered, and lock back into placed when raised. Check the condition of the rear parcel shelf.

Ensure the central locking system functions correctly by using the door key (driver's side only), and by using the internal locking button. Check that when the doors are locked the alarm system indicator light in the dash is flashing at a rate of one per second, once the alarm system has finished its self-test program. Rate the interior on overall condition, operation of all electrical and mechanical seat functions, central locking, alarm system indication and interior lighting operation.

Basic PDK steering wheel.
(Author's collection)

Steering wheel and horn
Inspect the airbag steering wheel for condition. Check horn operation. Rating is for steering wheel condition and horn operation.

Steering column control stalks
Check all steering column stalk functions. Rating is for condition of each stalk lever and its operation.

Instruments
The 2nd generation 997 model ranges were offered with numerous instrument dial and bezel colours, in various materials including aluminium, carbon fibre and wood. Check the option package before concluding anything is not original. Check each instrument's internal lighting is functioning correctly when the headlights are turned on, and check the light system dimming, the operation of which depends on installed options (check the owner's (driver's) manual). Rating is for instrument condition and correct internal lighting operation.

Warning lights
Consult the owner's (driver's) manual warning light system pages, as it's important to know what warning lights are fitted to a specific 997 model, and the warning and advisory lights are installed in numerous locations, including some switches. Engage the handbrake (parking, emergency brake) and turn on the ignition, but do not start the engine. The warning system electronics will illuminate; test all warning and advisory lights. Ensure all warning lights that should be illuminated are. If

Instrument warning and advisory lights illuminated. (Courtesy Porsche AG archive)

there any doubts, read the owner's manual again, or ask the seller about it. Rating is for condition of warning symbols and correct operation whilst the 997 is static.

The next stage is to put the 997 on to a lifter or over a pit and carry out some basic inspections from underneath.

Underside panels

Every road legal 997 is fitted with quite extensive underside panelling. Check all is present. Look for evidence of scrap marks or impact damage. Never purchase a 997 without its underside panels. Rating is for condition of panels and sealing.

It's time for lifting and inspecting underneath. (Courtesy Chip Witt)

That's a lot of panelling underneath. (Courtesy Chip Witt)

View from beneath. (Courtesy Chip Witt)

The 2nd generation exposed. (Courtesy Chip Witt)

It's easier to inspect the suspension and brakes from underneath. (Courtesy Chip Witt)

The entire exhaust system can also be inspected from underneath. (Courtesy David Yusem)

Suspension

All 997 models, except the GT models, have a non-adjustable suspension system. A visual inspection of the 997 from underneath should reveal any suspension issues. Check for any aftermarket modifications to the suspension. If in doubt, ask the seller about it. Rating is for suspension condition and aftermarket modifications.

Exhaust system

The 997 is not fitted with a rear engine cover, which ensures the entire exhaust system is easily inspected. Ask the seller if any exhaust modifications have been carried out. Rating is for exhaust system originality and condition.

Oil leaks

One of the best oil leak checks that can be carried out is done after the test drive. Park the 997 on level ground and slide some butcher's paper under the engine. Go away and come back after 30 to 60 minutes. Pull out the paper and check how much oil has fallen on to it. Rating is for any detected oil leaks during the static inspection and after the test drive.

Coolant leaks

Check the ground under the front spoiler, around each front wheel and around the rear left side of the engine bay for any evidence of radiator coolant leakage. Rating is based on any detected leaks.

Transmission fluid and water leaks

Inspect for any evidence of transmission fluid and water leaks from the washer system tank installed in the left side front fender (guard/wing). Most leaks can usually be detected in the vent holes of the underside panels. Rating is for detected transmission fluid and water leaks.

Test drive

This is mandatory. During the test drive, every system must be tested including the air-conditioning, heating, sound etc. Everything with a button must be switched on and tested. The test drive rating must reflect the correct function of every system, the car's handling, braking efficiency, acceleration, and gear changing – and the intensity of the smile on your face.

A test drive is mandatory. (Courtesy Porsche AG archive)

Don't play hardball with the seller.
(Courtesy David Yusem)

Playing hardball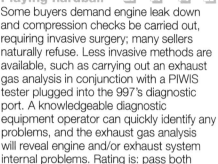

Some buyers demand engine leak down and compression checks be carried out, requiring invasive surgery; many sellers naturally refuse. Less invasive methods are available, such as carrying out an exhaust gas analysis in conjunction with a PIWIS tester plugged into the 997's diagnostic port. A knowledgeable diagnostic equipment operator can quickly identify any problems, and the exhaust gas analysis will reveal engine and/or exhaust system internal problems. Rating is: pass both tests, full points, failure of one or both, null point (no points) and walk away.

Evaluation procedure
Add up the points scored!

150 to 160 points = excellent to almost concours class, hope it doesn't break.

140 to 149 points = good to very good, but it's going to cost to keep it this way.

120 to 139 points = average to good, but where were the problems found?

110 to 119 points = below average to average, and careful consideration required.

100 to 109 points = border line money pit.

80 to 99 points = beware: it's going to cost a lot of money, what's the purchase price?

79 points or less = run away, unless you want to turn a big fortune into a small one.

If any 997 scores less than 100 from such a detailed inspection, the buyer needs to carefully consider their purchasing position, because it's definitely going to be a money pit. Restoration of such a complicated piece of machinery to full roadworthiness is a labour of love, as the money sunk into it cannot be recovered.

Rose-coloured glasses can obscure a multitude of sins, but these puppies are perfect 2nd generation 997 examples; top 1%. (Courtesy Wayne Smith and David Yusem)

10 Auctions
– sold! Another way to buy your dream

Auction pros & cons
Pros: Prices will usually be lower than those of dealers or private sellers and you might grab a real bargain on the day. Auctioneers have usually established clear title with the seller. At the venue you can usually examine documentation relating to the vehicle.
Cons: You have to rely on a sketchy catalogue description of condition & history. The opportunity to inspect is limited and you cannot drive the car. Auction cars are often a little below par and may require some work. It's easy to overbid. There will usually be a buyer's premium to pay in addition to the auction hammer price.

Which auction?
Auctions by established auctioneers are advertised in car magazines and on the auction houses' websites. A catalogue, or a simple printed list of the lots for auctions might only be available a day or two ahead, though often lots are listed and pictured on auctioneers' websites much earlier. Contact the auction company to ask if previous auction selling prices are available as this is useful information (details of past sales are often available on websites).

Catalogue, entry fee and payment details
When you purchase the catalogue of the vehicles in the auction, it often acts as a ticket allowing two people to attend the viewing days and the auction. Catalogue details tend to be comparatively brief, but will include information such as 'one owner from new, low mileage, full service history,' etc. It will also usually show a guide price to give you some idea of what to expect to pay and will tell you what is charged as a 'Buyer's premium.' The catalogue will also contain details of acceptable forms of payment. At the fall of the hammer an immediate deposit is usually required, the balance payable within 24 hours. If the plan is to pay by cash there may be a cash limit. Some auctions will accept payment by debit card. Sometimes credit or charge cards are acceptable, but will often incur an extra charge. A bank draft or bank transfer will have to be arranged in advance with your own bank as well as with the auction house. No car will be released before *all* payments are cleared. If delays occur in payment transfers then storage costs can accrue.

Buyer's premium
A buyer's premium will be added to the hammer price: *don't* forget this in your calculations. It is not usual for there to be a further state tax or local tax on the purchase price and/or on the buyer's premium.

Viewing
In some instances, it's possible to view on the day, or days before, as well as in the hours prior to, the auction. There are auction officials available who are willing to help out by opening engine and luggage compartment lids and to allow you to inspect the interior. While the officials may start the engine for you, a test drive is out of the question. Crawling under and around the car as much as you want is permitted, but

you can't suggest that the car you are interested in be jacked up, or attempt to do the job yourself. You can also ask to see any documentation available.

Bidding

Before you take part in the auction, *decide your maximum bid – and stick to it!*

It may take a while for the auctioneer to reach the lot you are interested in, so use that time to observe how other bidders behave. When it's the turn of your car, attract the auctioneer's attention and make an early bid. The auctioneer will then look to you for a reaction every time another bid is made; usually the bids will be in fixed increments until the bidding slows, when smaller increments will often be accepted before the hammer falls. If you want to withdraw from the bidding, make sure the auctioneer understands your intentions – a vigorous shake of the head when he or she looks to you for the next bid should do the trick! Assuming that you are the successful bidder, the auctioneer will note your card or paddle number, and from that moment on you will be responsible for the vehicle.

If the car is unsold, either because it failed to reach the reserve or because there was little interest, it may be possible to negotiate with the owner, via the auctioneers, after the sale is over.

Successful bid

There are two more items to think about. How to get the 997 home and insurance? If you can't drive the car, your own or a hired trailer is one way, another is to have the vehicle shipped using the facilities of a local company. The auction house will also have details of companies specialising in the transfer of cars.

Insurance for immediate cover can usually be purchased on site, but it may be more cost-effective to make arrangements with your own insurance company in advance, and then call to confirm the full details.

eBay & other online auctions

eBay & other online auctions could land you a 997 at a bargain price, though you'd be foolhardy to bid without examining the car first, something most vendors encourage. A useful feature of eBay is that the geographical location of the car is shown, so you can narrow your choices to those within a realistic radius of home. Be prepared to be outbid in the last few moments of the auction. Remember, your bid is binding and that it will be very, very difficult to get restitution in the case of a crooked vendor fleecing you – caveat emptor!

Be aware that some cars offered for sale in online auctions are 'ghost' cars. Don't part with any cash without being sure that the vehicle does actually exist and is as described (usually pre-bidding inspection is possible).

Auctioneers

Barrett-Jackson / www.barrett-jackson.com
Bonhams / www.bonhams.com
British Car Auctions BCA) / www.bca-europe.com or www.british-car-auctions.co.uk
Christies / www.christies.com Coys www.coys.co.uk

eBay / www.ebay.com
H&H / www.handh.co.uk
RM Sotheby's / www.rmsothebys.com
Shannons / www.shannons.com.au
Silver / www.silverauctions.com

11 Paperwork
– correct documentation is essential!

The paper trail

Porsche cars usually come with a large portfolio of paperwork accumulated and passed on by a succession of proud owners. This documentation represents the real history of the car and from it can be deduced the level of care the car has received, how much it's been used, which specialists have worked on it and the dates of major repairs and restorations. All of this information will be priceless to you as the new owner, so be very wary of cars with little paperwork to support their claimed history.

Registration documents

All countries/states have some form of registration for private vehicles whether it's like the American 'pink slip' system or the British 'log book' system.

It is essential to check that the registration document is genuine, that it relates to the car in question, and that all the vehicle's details are correctly recorded, including chassis/VIN and engine numbers (if these are shown). If you are buying from the previous owner, his or her name and address will be recorded in the document: this will not be the case if you are buying from a dealer.

In the UK the current (Euro-aligned) registration document is named 'V5C,' and is printed in coloured sections of blue, green and pink. The blue section relates to the car specification, the green section has details of the new owner and the pink section is sent to the DVLA in the UK when the car is sold. A small section in yellow deals with selling the car within the motor trade.

Roadworthiness certificate

Most country/state administrations require that vehicles are regularly tested to prove that they are safe to use on the public highway and do not produce excessive emissions. In the UK that test (the 'MOT') is carried out at approved testing stations, for a fee. In the USA the requirement varies, but most states insist on an emissions test every two years as a minimum, while the police are charged with pulling over unsafe-looking vehicles.

In the UK the test is required on an annual basis once a vehicle becomes three years old. Of particular relevance for older cars is that the certificate issued includes the mileage reading recorded at the test date and, therefore, becomes an independent record of that car's history. Ask the seller if previous certificates are available. Without an MOT the vehicle should be trailered to its new home, unless you insist that a valid MOT is part of the deal. (Not such a bad idea this, as at least you will know the car was roadworthy on the day it was tested and you don't need to wait for the old certificate to expire before having the test done.)

In the UK, vehicles over 40 years old on May 20th each year, are exempt from MOT testing. Owners can still have the test carried out if they so wish.

Road licence

The administration of every country/state charges some kind of tax for the use of its road system, the actual form of the 'road licence' and, how it is displayed, varying enormously country to country and state to state.

Whatever the form of the road licence, it must relate to the vehicle carrying it and must be present and valid if the car is to be driven on the public highway legally.

Changed legislation in the UK means that the seller of a car must surrender any existing road fund licence, and it is the responsibility of the new owner to re-tax the vehicle at the time of purchase and before the car can be driven on the road. It's therefore vital to see the Vehicle Registration Certificate (V5C) at the time of purchase, and to have access to the New Keeper Supplement (V5C/2), allowing the buyer to obtain road tax immediately.

In the UK, classic vehicles 40 years old or more on the 1st January each year get free road tax. It is still necessary to renew the tax status every year, even if there is no change.

If the car is untaxed because it has not been used for a period of time, the owner has to inform the licensing authorities.

Certificates of authenticity

For most Porsche models it is possible to obtain a certificate proving the age and authenticity (eg engine and chassis serial numbers, paint colour and trim). If you want to obtain one, the only place to start is with your local Porsche dealer, but there is a cost involved and in some countries it's not possible to obtain a Certificate of Authenticity.

If the car has been used in European classic car rallies it may have a FIVA (Federation Internationale des Vehicules Anciens) certificate. The so-called 'FIVA Passport,' or 'FIVA Vehicle Identity Card,' enables organisers and participants to recognise if a particular vehicle is suitable for individual events. To obtain such a certificate go to www.fbhvc.co.uk or www.fiva.org, or similar for other countries.

Service history

Enthusiastic capable owners have serviced their 2nd generation 997s at home instead of using dealer networks or recognised independent Porsche specialists. Nevertheless, try to obtain as much service history and other paperwork pertaining to the car as you can. Naturally, dealer stamps, or recognised specialist garage receipts score the most points in the value stakes. However, anything helps in the great authenticity game, items like the original bill of sale, handbook, parts invoices and repair bills, adding to the story and the character of the car. Even a brochure correct to the year of the car's manufacture is a useful document and something that you could well have to search hard to locate in future years. If the seller claims that the car has been restored, then expect receipts and other evidence from a specialist restorer.

If the seller claims to have carried out regular servicing, ask what work was completed, when, and seek some evidence of it being carried out. Your assessment of the car's overall condition should tell you whether the seller's claims are genuine.

Restoration photographs

If the seller tells you that the 997 is a restored example, then expect to be shown a series of photographs taken while the restoration was under way. Pictures taken at various stages, and from various angles, should help you gauge the thoroughness of the work. If you buy the car, ask if you can have all the photographs as they form an important part of the vehicle's history. It's surprising how many sellers are happy to part with their car and accept your cash, but want to hang on to their photographs! In the latter event, you may be able to persuade the vendor to get a set of copies made.

12 What's it worth?

– let your head rule your heart

Heart and head

I always believe you will know the right Porsche for you. It's the one that puts a permanent smile on your face and causes your heart to race like the first time you fell in love – but! This is a cruel world and you must not let your heart rule your head because, if you get it wrong, your heart will sink, and that may be just the start of your troubles.

Condition

If the car you've been looking at is really bad, then you've probably not bothered to use the marking system in Chapter 9 – 60 minute evaluation. You may not have even got as far as using that chapter at all!

If you did use the marking system in Chapter 9, you'll know whether the car is in Excellent (maybe Concours), Good, Average or Poor condition or, perhaps, somewhere in-between these categories. Many car magazines run a regular price guide. If you haven't bought the latest editions, do so now and compare their suggested values for the model you are thinking of buying: also look at the auction prices they're reporting. Values have been fairly stable for some time, but some models will always be more sought-after than others. Trends can change too. The values published in the magazines tend to vary from one magazine to another, as do their scales of condition, so read carefully the guidance notes they provide. Bear in mind that a car that is truly a recent show winner could be worth more than the highest scale published. Assuming that the car you have in mind is not in show/ concours condition, relate the level of condition that you judge the car to be in with the appropriate guide price. How does the figure compare with the asking price? Before you start haggling with the seller, consider what affect any variation from standard specification might have on the car's value. If you are buying from a dealer, remember there will be a dealer's premium (profit margin) on the price as they have to feed their families as well.

Desirable options/extras

All-leather interior
Porsche adaptive sports seats
Porsche Exclusive interior options
Porsche Exclusive exterior options
Sports exhaust
Bose surround sound system
Sport Chrono option

Undesirable features

Repainted and/or the original colour changed
Unapproved aftermarket wheels (incorrect size and offset)
Unapproved tyres
Noisy aftermarket exhaust modifications
Non-Porsche aerodynamic additions
Non-Porsche fibreglass or Kevlar panels

Stripped-out interior
Aftermarket flashed Siemens DME (ECU)

Warranty

Commercial car dealers have to provide a minimum period of warranty on certain items on any car, but in the real world is the warranty worth the paper it's written on? Look around; is this dealer capable of dealing with repairing sophisticated Porsche engineering? What's covered by the warranty? How far from the dealer do you live? How are you going to get the car back to the dealer? What about purchasing extended warranty policies? Ask yourself the same questions. Is the company underwriting the warranty policy going to be around in two years time? Warranty, unless purchasing from a reputable approved Porsche dealer, should not be a purchase consideration, as in the real world nine out of ten times when something fails it is not going to be repaired under any warranty scheme without a fight and more often than not the buyer loses. Maybe it might be worth getting a discount on the purchase price and foregoing the warranty altogether?

Private purchases are not protected by mandatory warranty requirements and getting a previous owner to pay for undisclosed problems and any repairs usually involves legal action.

Pre-purchase inspection

This buyer's guide contains many procedures that you as the buyer can follow, but I still strongly recommend that any 997 being seriously considered for purchase be taken to a recognised expert, usually a Porsche dealer for a fully independent inspection. A PPI should also detect any legal issues such as forged registration papers. Ringing of VINs or detecting clones of legally registered cars does require expertise, but nothing is ever guaranteed. You will have to pay for such an inspection, but it's worth it.

Striking a deal

Negotiate on the basis of your condition assessment, mileage, and fault rectification cost. Also take into account the car's specification. Be realistic about the value, but don't be completely intractable: a small compromise on the part of the vendor or buyer will often facilitate a deal at little real cost. However, it's critical that you use your evaluation points score as your basis for negotiating the price down. If you have identified problems that from this guide or from other sources you know are going to cost a lot of money to rectify, you must insist these costs are deducted from the final purchase price. Just one failed electronic unit can cost over ●x2000, so why pay for it if you already know it's failed? It's far better to walk away from a deal than to let your heart rule your head. There is always a better deal out there somewhere.

www.velocebooks.com / www.veloce.co.uk
Details of all current books • New book news • Special offers • Gift vouchers • Forum

46

13 Do you really want to restore?

– it'll take longer and cost more than you think

A Porsche 997 is not a normal 'car' and does not have the more traditional separate chassis and body assembly. Its monocoque (unibody) construction is an extremely complicated piece of design and engineering. It's very difficult to pull apart, repair and put back together properly. The biggest issues with structural repair of the 997's unibody are: getting all the right parts; jigging and clamping them into the correct position; and welding accurately and treating the metalwork (including the weld joints) to ensure that rust cannot form in, and around, the repair during the restoration and/or after it has all been painted.

Specialist tools and equipment, including a proper assembly jig, is required for all structural repairs, as is the factory workshop structural repair manual, which must be followed to the letter. There are no short cuts when the objective is to properly repair the 997's structure.

Electrical and electronics systems installed in the 997 are complicated and components such as system control units extremely expensive to purchase, and, in some cases, hard to find. There are almost no 997 electronic control unit repair facilities in the world. Replacement is the only option for most people. Any damaged 997 wiring loom is a nightmare to repair.

In summary, the Porsche 997 is a piece of precision engineering, and does not lend itself easily to major restoration, but, if you are not convinced, read on, Macduff.

Questions and answers
• The biggest cost in any restoration is labour: can you do it all yourself or do you need professional help?
• How are your welding and painting skills?
• Do you have the required tooling and specialist equipment including a monocoque jig for any structural repairs?
• Do you have the Porsche workshop structural repair manual?
• Do you have the facilities?
• Do you have an approved Porsche dealer nearby?
• Do you have the time?
• What are your time expectations for the job? Your dedication is high now, but what's it going to be in two years time?
• If you cannot do the work yourself, can you afford professional restoration? A full external and internal restoration including engine and transmission rebuilds is going to cost a huge amount in any currency.
• Is a rolling chassis restoration an option? Good luck in finding one.
• In theory, if a full 'nut & bolt' restoration is intended, it's usually best to buy the worst car you can find, so long as certain components are good, but how will you know what's good and what's not, without specialist test equipment and knowledge?
• Will the money ploughed into a full restoration ever be recovered? Not a chance. In the Porsche world originality is always worth more than restored.

A 997 restoration can only be approached as a labour of love, as it makes no economic sense.

Potential Carrera 4S Cabriolet restoration project ... (Author's collection)

... exterior ... (Author's collection)

... engine bay. (Author's collection)

... interior ...
(Author's collection)

... ditto ...
(Author's collection)

... ditto.
(Author's collection)

14 Paint problems
– bad complexion, including dimples, pimples and bubbles

Paint faults generally occur due lack of protection and/or maintenance, or to poor preparation prior to a repaint or touch-up. Some of the following conditions may be present in the car you're looking at:

Orange peel (bad)

Most 997s leave the factory with a slight orange peel look. However, bad orange peel is an uneven paint surface, similar to the appearance of the skin of an orange. The fault is caused by the failure of atomized paint droplets to flow into each other when they hit the surface. It's sometimes possible to rub out the effect with proprietary paint cutting/rubbing compound or very fine grades of abrasive paper. A repaint may be necessary in severe cases. Consult a bodywork repairer/paint shop for advice on the particular car.

On the way to the paint shop ...
(Courtesy Porsche AG archive)

... painting ... (Courtesy Porsche AG archive)

... always resulted in a slight orange peel effect. (Courtesy Porsche AG archive)

Measuring paint depth. (Courtesy Porsche AG archive)

Cracking

Severe cases are likely to have been caused by too heavy an application of paint (or filler beneath the paint). Also, insufficient stirring of the paint before application can lead to the components being improperly mixed, and cracking can result. Incompatibility with the paint already on the panel can have a similar effect. To rectify the problem, it is necessary to rub down to a smooth, sound finish before repainting the problem area. Rolling of fenders (guards or wings) can also cause cracking.

Crazing

Sometimes the paint takes on a crazed rather than a cracked appearance when the problems mentioned under 'Cracking' are present. This problem can also be caused by a reaction between the underlying surface and the paint. Paint removal and repainting the problem area is usually the only solution. Painted thermal plastics will craze over time.

Speedster custom blue exterior paint.
(Courtesy Porsche AG archive)

Black Edition exterior paint.
(Courtesy Porsche AG archive)

Blistering
Is very rare, but, when it does occur on the 997, it's always caused by rust developing underneath the paint. Usually perforation will be found in the metal and the damage will usually be worse than that suggested by the area of blistering. The metal will have to be repaired before repainting.

Micro blistering
Usually the result of an economic repaint. Consult a paint specialist, but usually damaged paint will have to be removed before partial or full repaint.

Fading and oxidation
Some colours, especially solid reds, are prone to fading and oxidation if subjected to strong sunlight for long periods without polish protection. Sometimes proprietary paint restorers and/or paint cutting/rubbing compounds will retrieve the situation. Often a repaint is the only real solution.

Peeling
Often a problem with metallic paintwork begins when the sealing lacquer becomes damaged and begins to peel off. Poorly applied paint may also peel. The remedy is to strip and start again!

Dimples
Dimples in the paintwork are caused by the residue of polish (particularly silicone types) not being removed properly before repainting. Paint removal and repainting is the only solution.

Dents
Small dents are usually easily cured by the 'Dentmaster,' or equivalent process, that sucks or pushes out the dent (as long as the paint surface is still intact). Companies offering dent removal services usually come to your home: consult your telephone directory.

15 Problems due to lack of use

– just like their owners, 997s need exercise!

Dolly Parton was asked once why she was still working as hard as ever in the music industry. She answered: "I'd rather wear out than rust out." Letting a 997 stand unused will ensure it rusts out rather than being worn out.

So what can happen if a 997 is not used and just sits?

Internal corrosion
Most commonly available 2nd generation 997s are fitted with what Porsche AG calls its internal dry-sump horizontally opposed flat-6 direct fuel-injection engine. This means that most of the oil is stored in an internal oil tank when the engine is switched off. Conversely, 2nd generation 997 GT models are still fitted with dry-sump flat-6 engines; the oil in these models is stored in an external tank when the engine is switched off. The result of both these oil storage methods is that the only protection against the onset of corrosion is the oil film left on the components. Over time gravity takes over, and the oil film drains away into the heads,

Corrosion has set in on this PDK transmission (997 Turbo). (Author's collection)

exposing bare metal to the environment. Over a long period of lack of use, corrosion will start. And there's another problem: oil starts to break down (separates into various chemical compounds). Depending on the type of oil used, some of those compounds will recombine, forming an acidic residue which corrodes any exposed metal it comes in contact with. Modern petrol blends with an ethanol content of more than 10% will also cause internal corrosion of the fuel delivery system right up to the fuel injectors. Corroded fuel manifold lines can result in a fuel leak and fire when the engine starts.

Seized components
Pistons in brake callipers will seize, this is caused by corrosion as the dust caps and seals dry out, crack and fail. Moisture in brake fluid used in the integrated brake system and for clutch actuation (except the Turbo) will start corrosion. All components are affected and all will eventually seize, causing horrendous problems when the 997 is powered up.

Brake pads may stick to the brake discs (rotors) regardless of type. Grey cast iron brake discs (rotors) will rust. The clutch may seize if the plate becomes stuck to the flywheel because of corrosion. The handbrake (parking or emergency brake) will seize as cables and linkages rust. In the 997 the handbrake assembly is installed in the rear wheel hubs and is quite complicated, and yes, expensive to repair.

Internal seals
Without fluid for lubrication, even synthetic rubber seals will start to dry out and break down. 2nd generation 997 DFI engines all use a large amount of o-rings and gaskets. Long-term storage without due care and attention will result in many oil leaks once the car's started again. The same issue applies in the braking system.

External seals
As time passes, all the rubber sealing used to protect the 997 against water ingress will harden, crack and fail.

Fluids

Old acidic engine oil will corrode any exposed metal it can get to. Brake fluid absorbs water from the atmosphere and must be renewed every two years. Untreated water left in the windscreen (windshield) washer system will stagnate.

Tyres and wheels

Tyres that have borne the weight of the car in the same position for some time will develop flat spots, resulting in driving vibrations. The tyre walls may develop cracks or (blister-type) bulges, and aged rubber can become too hard and unsafe. Corroded 5-bolt or centre-lock wheels are expensive to repair, and/or replace.

MacPherson struts and shock absorbers (dampers)

With lack of use, the dampers' seals will fail, allowing the gas used as part of the internal damping system to escape, and the dampers will collapse. 997s with Porsche active suspension management (PASM) installed will be very expensive to repair, if the front struts and/or rear shock absorbers are leaking.

Rubber and plastic

Rubber is used throughout the 997 in various mounts for the transmission and suspension, and in bushings. Once it goes hard and cracks, all sorts of grunts, groans, vibrations and, in the worst-case scenario, handling problems, can occur. Fuel hoses are made from rubber, as are many of the engine oil system interconnects. Once these hoses perish there is a serious risk of fire. Half (drive) shaft CV joints and steering arms have rubber covers (boots) and, when these crack, it allows the outside environment into sensitive lubricated components, which will eventually fail.

Electrics

Leaving a battery installed and not driving the 997 will result in it going completely flat in under four weeks; in winter it will die more quickly. A lead acid battery left discharged for long periods will not be capable of being charged, and must be replaced. Earth/grounding problems are common on the 997 when the connections have corroded. Sparkplugs will corrode, but the 997 has no sparkplug leads or distributor system to worry about. However, rodents looking for food – and a new home – may target exposed wiring.

Rotting exhaust system

Exhaust gas always contains some water, which is generated in the catalytic converter. Water sitting for long periods of time in a cold exhaust system will cause it to rot from the inside. External areas of the exhaust system will also rust, due to corrosive elements in the atmosphere, or salt and other road grime.

Mould

Most 997s have a partial if not full leather interior. The right environmental conditions will allow moisture inside the car to become mould growing in the leather, and spreading throughout the entire interior and the luggage compartment.

16 The Community

– key people, organisations and companies in the 997 world

This chapter provides various sources for prospective 997 owners to find advice and guidance, what's available to read, and who to join up with if a purchase is made. The 997 series has a huge and enthusiastic following around the world, and, if you purchase a 997, you will also join the larger rear engine 911 community.

Books
Porsche 997 The Essential Companion: Porsche Excellence by Adrian Streather published by Veloce Publishing. ISBN: 978-1-845846-20-6

Magazines
Look for back issues of UK magazines *Total911*, *GT Porsche* and *911 Porsche World* or the USA's *Excellence* and *Panorama* publications. Whilst there is no specific 997 magazine, there are many periodicals that report fairly and often on the series.

Porsche major assembly rebuild and/or service
Callas Rennsport
19080 Hawthorne Blvd
Torrance
California 90503
USA
Tel: +1 310 370 7038
www.callasrennsport.com

Porsche parts suppliers
Porsche Centre Hatfield
1 Hatfield Avenue
Hatfield Business Park
Hatfield
Hertfordshire
AL10 9UA
England
Tel: +44 (0) 1707 277911
https://www.porschehatfield.co.uk

Porsch Apart Ltd
Unit 4 Field Mill
Harrison Street
Ramsbottom
Bury
Lancashire
BL0 0AH
England
Tel: +44 (0) 1706 824053
www.porsch-apart.co.uk

Porsche clubs

The author has been involved with some Porsche clubs in the past and is happy to recommend:

http://www.pcsa.asn.au/
Porsche Club of South Australia
PCSA Inc.
PO Box 2209
Kent Town
South Australia 5071
Australia

http://www.porscheclubgb.com/
Porsche Club Great Britain registered office
Cornbury House
Cotswold Business Village, London Road
Moreton-in-Marsh
Gloucestershire
GL56 0JQ
England
Tel: +44 (0)1608 652911

http://www.tipec.net/ (The Independent Porsche Enthusiasts Club)
TIPEC Club Office
10 Whitecroft Gardens
Woodford Halse
Northants
NN11 3PY
England
Tel: +44 (0) 8456 020052

Internet-based Porsche communities

For North American readers, please check the Porsche Club America website www.pca.org to find the contact address of the PCA region nearest to you.

Google is your friend. There are many internet-based Porsche communities in almost every country in the world. Use the search words 'Porsche 997' to get started or check out:

http://www.porschemania.it/ Italian Porsche enthusiasts highly recommended.
http://www.porschetuningmag.com lots of great information in English.

www.velocebooks.com / www.veloce.co.uk
Details of all current books • New book news • Special offers • Gift vouchers • Forum

54

17 Vital statistics

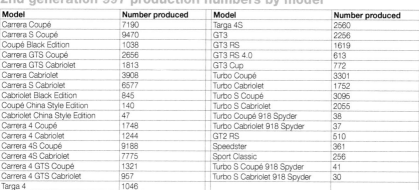

– essential data at your fingertips

2nd generation 997 production numbers by model

Model	Number produced	Model	Number produced
Carrera Coupé	7190	Targa 4S	2560
Carrera S Coupé	9470	GT3	2256
Coupé Black Edition	1038	GT3 RS	1619
Carrera GTS Coupé	2656	GT3 RS 4.0	613
Carrera GTS Cabriolet	1813	GT3 Cup	772
Carrera Cabriolet	3908	Turbo Coupé	3301
Carrera S Cabriolet	6577	Turbo Cabriolet	1752
Cabriolet Black Edition	845	Turbo S Coupé	3095
Coupé China Style Edition	140	Turbo S Cabriolet	2055
Cabriolet China Style Edition	47	Turbo Coupé 918 Spyder	38
Carrera 4 Coupé	1748	Turbo Cabriolet 918 Spyder	37
Carrera 4 Cabriolet	1244	GT2 RS	510
Carrera 4S Coupé	9188	Speedster	361
Carrera 4S Cabriolet	7775	Sport Classic	256
Carrera 4 GTS Coupé	1321	Turbo S Coupé 918 Spyder	41
Carrera 4 GTS Cabriolet	957	Turbo S Cabriolet 918 Spyder	30
Targa 4	1046		
Total			76,259
Total combined 997 series production			**212,704**

2nd generation 997 model type numbers

Model	Type number	Engine type number	Model years by 10th VIN digit identification
Carrera Coupé (LHD)	997 110	MA1.02	9, A, B
Carrera Coupé (RHD)	997 111	MA1.02	9, A, B
Carrera S Coupé (LHD)	997 120	MA1.01	9, A, B
Carrera S Coupé (RHD)	997 121	MA1.01	9, A, B
Carrera Cabriolet (LHD)	997 310	MA1.02	9, A, B
Carrera Cabriolet (RHD)	997 311	MA1.02	9, A, B
Carrera S Cabriolet (LHD)	997 320	MA1.01	9, A, B
Carrera S Cabriolet (RHD)	997 321	MA1.01	9, A, B
Carrera 4 Coupé (LHD)	997 410	MA1.02	9, A, B, C
Carrera 4 Coupé (RHD)	997 411	MA1.02	9, A, B, C
Carrera 4S Coupé (LHD)	997 430	MA1.01	9, A, B, C
Carrera 4S Coupé (RHD)	997 431	MA1.01	9, A, B, C
Carrera 4 Cabriolet (LHD)	997 610	MA1.02	9, A, B, C
Carrera 4 Cabriolet (RHD)	997 611	MA1.02	9, A, B, C
Carrera 4S Cabriolet (LHD)	997 620	MA1.01	9, A, B, C
Carrera 4S Cabriolet (RHD)	997 621	MA1.01	9, A, B, C
Targa 4 (LHD)	997 510	MA1.02	9, A, B, C
Targa 4 (RHD)	997 511	MA1.02	9, A, B, C
Targa 4S (LHD)	997 520	MA1.01	9, A, B, C
Targa 4S (RHD)	997 521	MA1.01	9, A, D, O
GT3 (LHD)	997 810	M97.77	A, B
GT3 (RHD)	997 811	M97.77	A, B
GT3 RS (LHD)	997 850	M97.77R	A, B
GT3 RS (RHD)	997 851	M97.77R	A, B
GT3 RS 4.0-litre (LHD)	997 880	M97.74	B, C
GT3 RS 4.0-litre (RHD)	997 881	M97.74	B, C
Turbo Coupé (LHD)	997 420	MA1.70	A, B, C, D
Turbo Coupé (RHD)	997 421	MA1.70	A, B, C, D
Turbo S Coupé (LHD)	997 450	MA1.70	B, C, D
Turbo S Coupé (RHD)	997 451	MA1.70	B, C, D
Turbo S Coupé 918 Spyder (LHD)	997 470	MA1.70S	B, C
Turbo S Coupé 918 Spyder (RHD)	997 471	MA1.70S	B, C

Model	Type number	Engine type number	Model years by 10th VIN digit identification
Turbo Cabriolet (LHD)	997 630	MA1.70	A, B, C, D
Turbo Cabriolet (RHD)	997 631	MA1.70	A, B, C, D
Turbo S Cabriolet (LHD)	997 650	MA1.70	B, C, D
Turbo S Cabriolet (RHD)	997 651	MA1.70	B, C, D
Turbo S Cabriolet 918 Spyder (LHD)	997 670	MA1.70S	B, C
Turbo S Cabriolet 918 Spyder (RHD)	997 671	MA1.70S	B, C
GT2 RS (LHD)	997 860	M97.70S	B, C
GT2 RS (RHD)	997 861	M97.70S	B, C
Sport Classic (LHD)	997 140	MA1.01S	A
Sport Classic (RHD)	997 141	MA1.01S	A
Carrera GTS Coupé (LHD)	997 150	MA1.01S	B, C
Carrera GTS Coupé (RHD)	997 151	MA1.01S	B, C
Carrera GTS Cabriolet (LHD)	997 350	MA1.01S	B, C
Carrera GTS Cabriolet (RHD)	997 351	MA1.01S	B, C
Carrera 4 GTS Coupé (LHD)	997 480	MA1.01S	B, C
Carrera 4 GTS Coupé (RHD)	997 481	MA1.01S	B, C
Carrera 4 GTS Cabriolet (LHD)	997 680	MA1.01S	B, C
Carrera 4 GTS Cabriolet (RHD)	997 681	MA1.01S	B, C
Carrera Black Edition Coupé (LHD)	997 160	MA1.02	B
Carrera Black Edition Coupé (RHD)	997 161	MA1.02	B
Carrera Black Edition Cabriolet (LHD)	997 360	MA1.02	B
Carrera Black Edition Cabriolet (RHD)	997 361	MA1.02	B
Speedster (LHD)	997 720	MA1.01S	A, B
Speedster (RHD)	997 721	MA1.01S	A, B
Carrera Coupé China Edition	997 170	MA1.02	A, B, C
Carrera Cabriolet China Edition	997 370	MA1.02	A, B, C

Normally-aspirated engine specifications

2nd generation 997 3.6-litre engine specifications	
Engine type	**MA1.02**
Bore mm/in	97/3.82
Stroke mm/in	81.5/3.2
Displacement cc/in^3	3614/220.5
Compression ratio	12.5:1
Engine power kW/hp	254/345 at 6500rpm
Engine torque Nm/lb-ft	390/289 at 4400rpm
Idle speed rpm manual Idle speed rpm PDK	680+/-80 680+/-80
Maximum cutoff rpm	7500
Fuel grade RON/CLC or AKI	recommended 98/93 minimum 95/90
Oil pressure @5000rpm @90°C/194°F	5 bar (72.5psi)
Maximum oil capacity litres/quarts	10.5/11.1
Maximum allowable oil consumption	1.5 litres per 1000km (1.6 quarts per 622 miles)

2nd generation 997 3.8-litre engine specifications (excluding GT3)		
Engine type	**MA1.01**	**MA1.01S**
Bore mm/in	102/4.01	
Stroke mm/in	77.5/3.05	
Displacement cc/in^3	3800/231.89	
Compression ratio	12.5:1	
Engine power kW/hp	283/385 at 6500rpm	
Engine torque Nm/lb-ft	420/311 at 4400rpm	
Idle speed rpm manual Idle speed rpm PDK	680+/-80 680+/-80	
Maximum cutoff rpm	7500	
Fuel grade RON/CLC or AKI	recommended 98/93 minimum 95/90	
Oil pressure @5000rpm @90°C/194°F	5 bar (72.5psi)	
Maximum oil capacity litres/quarts	10.5/11.1	
Maximum allowable oil consumption	1.5 litres per 1000km (1.6 quarts per 622 miles)	

2nd generation 997 3.8-litre engine specifications GT3 and GT3 RS only		
Engine type	M97.77	M97.77R
Bore mm/in	102.7/4.04	
Stroke mm/in	76.4/3.01	
Displacement cc/in^3	3797/231.6	
Compression ratio	12.0:1	12.2:1
Engine power kW/hp	320/435 at 7600rpm	450/331 at 7900rpm
Engine torque Nm/lb-ft	430/317 at 6250rpm	430/317 at 6250rpm
Idle speed rpm	720+/-40	
Maximum cutoff rpm	8500	
Fuel grade RON/CLC or AKI	recommended 98/93 minimum 95/90	
Oil pressure @5000rpm @90°C/194°F	7 bar (101.5psi)	
Maximum oil capacity litres/quarts	12/12.7	
Maximum allowable oil consumption	1.5 litres per 1000km (1.6 quarts per 622 miles)	
Engine weight manual kg/lb	183/403.5	

2nd generation 997 4.0-litre engine specifications GT3 RS only	
Engine type	M97.74
Bore mm/in	102.7/4.04
Stroke mm/in	80.4/3.2
Displacement cc/in^3	3996/243.9
Compression ratio	12.6:1
Engine power kW/hp	368/500 at 8250rpm
Engine torque Nm/lb-ft	460/339 at 5750rpm
Idle speed rpm	720+/-40
Maximum rpm (fuel shut-off)	8500
Fuel grade RON/CLC or AKI	recommended 98/93 minimum 95/90
Oil pressure @5000rpm @90°C/194°F	7 bar (101.5psi)
Maximum oil capacity litres/quarts	12/12.7
Maximum allowable oil consumption	1.5 litres per 1000km (1.6 quarts per 622 miles)
Engine weight kg/lb	181/399

Turbocharged engine specifications

2nd generation 997 3.8-litre turbocharged engine specifications		
Engine type	MA1.70	MA1.70S
Bore mm/in	102/4.016	
Stroke mm/in	77.5/3.051	
Displacement cc/in^3	3800/231.9	
Compression ratio	9.8:1	
Engine power kW/hp	368/500 at 6000rpm	390/523 at 6250 – 6750rpm
Engine torque Nm/lb-ft	650/480 at 1950 – 5000 rpm 700/516 over boost at 2000 – 4500rpm	700/516 at 2100 – 4250
Idle speed rpm manual Idle speed rpm PDK	680+/-25 680+/-25	Not applicable 680+/-25
Maximum cutoff rpm	7000	
Maximum factory set boost	0.8 bar (11.6psi)	1 bar/14.5psi
Fuel grade RON/CLC or AKI	recommended 98/93 minimum 95/90	
Oil pressure @5000rpm @90°C/194°F	6.5 bar (94psi)	
Maximum oil capacity litres/quarts	10.5/11.1	
Maximum allowable oil consumption	1.5 litres per 1000km (1.6 quarts per 622 miles)	
Engine weight PDK kg/lb	217/478.4	

6-speed manual transmission types

6-speed manual transmission applications			
Transmission type	Engine type	Model application(s)	Remarks
G97.05	MA1.02	Carrera model range all bodystyles	2nd generation
G97.35	MA1.02	Carrera 4 model range all bodystyles	2nd generation
G97.05	MA1.01	Carrera S model range all bodystyles	2nd generation
G97.35	MA1.01	Carrera 4S model range all bodystyles	2nd generation
G97.55	MA1.70	Turbocharged model range except GT2	2nd generation
G97.90	M97.77	GT3 and GT3 RS	2nd generation
G97.92	M97.77R	GT3 RS	2nd generation
G97.92	M97.74	GT3 RS 4.0-litre	2nd generation

7-speed Porsche Doppelkupplung (PDK) transmission types

7-speed PDK transmission applications			
Transmission type	Engine type	Model application(s)	Remarks
CG1.00	MA1.02	Carrera model range all bodystyles	2nd generation
CG1.30	MA1.02	Carrera 4 model range all bodystyles	2nd generation
CG1.00	MA1.01	Carrera S model range all bodystyles	2nd generation
CG1.30	MA1.01	Carrera 4S model range all bodystyles	2nd generation
CG1.50	MA1.70	Turbocharged model range except GT2	2nd generation

Brake system specifications all 997 series

Model	Carrera, Carrera 4 and Targa 4	Carrera S	Carrera 4S and Targa 4S	Turbo	GT3 and GT3 RS	GT2 and PCCB option
Brake boost system						
Booster servo assist	Vacuum					
Booster type	10 inch single	9 inch tandem				
Boost factor ratio	4.5	5.5				
Rear brake proportioning						
Method	Electronic					
Brake calliper						
Type front	4-piston monobloc	6-piston monobloc	6-piston aluminium monobloc			
Type rear	4-piston monobloc	4-piston aluminium monobloc				
Standard brake disc (rotor) front and rear						
Type	Grey cast iron	Carbon composite				
Brake disc (rotor) diameter, mm (in)						
Front	318 (12.52)	330 (12.99)	380 (14.96)	350 (13.78)	380 (14.96)	
Rear	299 (11.77)	330 (12.99)	350 (13.78)			
Brake disc (rotor) thickness, mm (in)						
Front	28 (1.10)	34 (1.34)				
Rear	24 (0.94)	28 (1.10)				

2nd generation brake system specifications variations

Model	Carrera, Carrera 4 and Targa 4	Carrera S	Carrera 4S and Targa 4S	Turbo	GT3 and GT3 RS	GT2 RS Turbo, Turbo S and option
Brake calliper						
Type front	4-piston aluminium fixed	No change	No change	6-piston aluminium monobloc		
Type rear	4-piston aluminium fixed	No change	No change	4-piston aluminium monobloc		
Brake disc (rotor) diameter, mm (in)						
Front	330 (12.99)	No change	No change	No change	380 (14.96)	
Rear	330 (12.99)	No change	No change	350 (13.78)		
Brake disc (rotor) thickness, mm (in)						
Front	34 (1.34)	No change	34 (1.34)			
Rear	28 (1.10)	No change	28 (1.10)			

Model dimensions

Model	Length mm (in)	Width* mm (in)	Height mm (in)	Front track width mm (in)	Rear track width mm (in)	Wheelbase mm (in)
Carrera	4466 (175.8)	1808 (71.2)	1310 (51.6)	1486 (58.5)	1534 (60.4)	2360 (92.9)
Carrera S	4466 (175.8)	1808 (71.2)	1300 (51.2)	1486 (58.5)	1534 (60.4)	2350 (92.5)
Carrera GTS	4466 (175.8)	1808 (71.2)	1300 (51.2)	1486 (58.5)	1534 (60.4)	2350 (92.5)
Carrera 4 & Targa 4	4466 (175.8)	1852 (72.9)	1310 (51.6)	1488 (58.6)	1548 (60.9)	2360 (92.9)
Carrera 4S & Targa 4S	4466 (175.8)	1852 (72.9)	1300 (51.2)	1488 (58.6)	1548 (60.9)	2350 (92.5)
Carrera 4 GTS	4466 (175.8)	1852 (72.9)	1300 (51.2)	1488 (58.6)	1548 (60.9)	2350 (92.5)
Turbo & Turbo S	4450 (175.3)	1852 (72.9)	1300 (51.2)	1490 (58.66)	1548 (60.9)	2350 (92.5)

Basic model empty weights
Manual transmission

Weight specification (EU 98/45/EC) kg (lb)	Carrera	Carrera S & GTS	Carrera 4 Targa 4	Carrera 4S Targa 4S & 4 GTS	Turbo
Curb (Kerb) weight Coupé	1490 (3285)	1500 (3307)	1540 (3395)	1555 (3428)	1645 (3627)
Curb (Kerb) weight Cabriolet	1575 (3472)	1585 (3494)	1630 (3594)	1640 (3616)	1720 (3792)
Curb (Kerb) weight Targa	n/a	n/a	1605 (3538)	1615 (3560)	n/a
Maximum roof rack load	75 (165)				

PDK transmission

Weight specification (EU 98/45/EC) kg (lb)	Carrera	Carrera S & GTS	Carrera 4 Targa 4	Carrera 4S Targa 4S & 4 GTS	Turbo
Curb (Kerb) weight Coupé	1520 (3351)	1550 (3417)	1575 (3472)	1585 (3494)	1670 (3682)
Curb (Kerb) weight Cabriolet	1605 (3538)	1615 (3560)	1660 (3660)	1670 (3682)	1745 (3847)
Curb (Kerb) weight Targa	n/a	n/a	1635 (3605)	1645 (3627)	n/a
Maximum roof rack load	75 (165)				

Manual transmission

Weight specification (EU 98/45/EC) kg (lb)	GT3	GT3 RS	GT2 RS
Curb (Kerb) weight Coupé	1395 (3075)	1375 (3031)	1445 (3186)
Maximum roof rack load	75 (165)		

Approved tyres

Approved summer tyre size combinations		
Tyre manufacturer, brand & N-rating		**Model and/or remarks**
235 40 ZR 18 (91Y) front and 265 40 ZR 18 (101Y) rear	Bridgestone Potenza RE050A N1	Carrera
	Continental SportContact 3 N1	Carrera
	Michelin Pilot Sport 2 N4	Carrera
235 35 ZR 19 (87Y) front and 295 30 ZR 19 (102Y) rear	Bridgestone Potenza RE050A N1	Carrera and S
	Michelin Pilot Sport 2 N2	Carrera and S
	Pirelli P Zero N2	Carrera and S
235 35 ZR 19 (87Y) front and 305 30 ZR 19 (102Y) rear	Bridgestone Potenza RE050A N1	Carrera, S, GTS, Sport Classic and Speedster
	Michelin Pilot Sport 2 N2	Carrera, S, GTS, Sport Classic and Speedster
	Pirelli P Zero N2	Carrera, S, GTS, Sport Classic and Speedster
235 40 ZR 18 (91Y) front and 295 35 ZR 18 (99Y) rear	Bridgestone Potenza RE050A N1	Carrera 4 and Targa 4
	Michelin Pilot Sport 2 N4	Carrera 4 and Targa 4
	Yokohama Advan Sport V103S N1	Carrera 4 and Targa 4
235 35 ZR 19 (87Y) front and 305 30 ZR 19 (102Y) rear	Bridgestone Potenza RE050A N1	Carrera 4, 4S, 4 GTS and Targa 4S
	Michelin Pilot Sport 2 N2	Carrera 4, 4S, 4 GTS and Targa 4S
	Pirelli P Zero N2	Carrera 4, 4S 4 GTS and Targa 4S
235 35 ZR 19 (87Y) front and 305 30 ZR 19 (102Y)	Michelin Pilot Sport Cup N1	GT3 and GT3 RS
235 35 ZR 19 (91Y) front and 305 30 ZR 19 (102Y)	Pirelli P Zero Corsa N0	GT3 and GT3 RS
	Pirelli P Zero Corsa N1	GT3 and GT3 RS
245 35 ZR 19 (89Y) front and 325 30 ZR 19 (101Y)	Michelin Pilot Sport Cup N1	GT3 and GT3 RS

Approved summer tyre size combinations		
Tyre manufacturer, brand & N-rating		**Model and/or remarks**
235 35 ZR 19 (87Y) front and 305 30 ZR 19 (102Y) rear	Michelin Pilot Sport Cup N0	Ultra high-performance for all models
235 35 ZR 19 (87Y) front and 305 30 ZR 19 (102Y)	Pirelli P Zero Rosso N1	Turbo and Turbo S
	Bridgestone Potenza RE050A N1	Turbo and Turbo S
	Michelin Pilot Sport 2 N2	Turbo and Turbo S
	Pirelli P Zero N2	Turbo and Turbo S
245 35 ZR 19 (89Y) front and 325 30 ZR 19 (101Y) rear	Michelin Pilot Sport Cup N1	GT2 RS front only
	Michelin Pilot Sport Cup N2	GT2 RS rear only

Approved winter tyres		
Manufacturer, model, N-rating		**Models and/or remarks**
235 40 R18 91V front and 265 40 R18 97V rear	Pirelli Winter 240 Sottozero Serie II N1	Carrera and S
	Continental Winter Contact TS810 N1	Carrera, S, GTS, SC and Speedster
	Michelin Pilot Alpin PA2 N2	Carrera, S, GTS, SC and Speedster
235 35 R18 91V front and 295 30 R18 97V rear	Pirelli Winter 240 Sottozero Serie II N2	Carrera, S, GTS, SC and Speedster
235 35 R18 91V front and 295 30 R18 99V rear	Pirelli Winter 240 Sottozero Serie II N1	All 997 models
	Nokian WR N0	All 997 models
235 35 R19 87V front and 30 R19 100V rear	Pirelli Winter 240 Sottozero Serie II N1	All 997 models
	Nokian WR N0	All 997 models except GT2 and RS

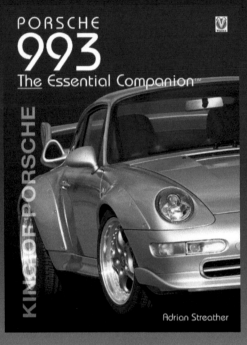

Index